17/6
15/9

The Engineers and the Price System

QMC   338170 7

a3021

MA...
QUEEN MARY, UNIVERSITY OF LONDON
Mile End Road, London E1 4NS
DATE DUE FOR RETURN

D1437901

The Engineers and the Price System

Thorstein Veblen

The Engineers and

A Harbinger Book

the Price System

WITH A NEW INTRODUCTION BY Daniel Bell

WITHDRAWN
FROM STOCK
QMUL LIBRARY

HARCOURT, BRACE & WORLD, INC.

NEW YORK • BURLINGAME

131166

HD 69.T4

© 1963 Harcourt, Brace & World, Inc.

Copyright 1921 B. W. Huebsch, Inc.
Renewed 1948 Ann B. Sims and Becky Meyers.
This edition published by arrangement with
The Viking Press, Inc.

Library of Congress Catalog Card No.: 63-19639

Printed in the United States of America

QUEEN MARY
COLLEGE
LIBRARY

Contents

INTRODUCTION TO THE HARBINGER EDITION
by Daniel Bell   1

I.   On the Nature and Uses of Sabotage   37

II. The Industrial System and the
     Captains of Industry   55

III. The Captains of Finance and
     the Engineers   71

IV. On the Danger of a Revolutionary
     Overturn   93

V.   On the Circumstances which Make
     for a Change   109

VI. A Memorandum on a Practicable
     Soviet of Technicians   131

Introduction
to the
Harbinger Edition

BY *Daniel Bell*

Periodically, there is a renewed wave of interest in Thorstein Veblen's *The Engineers and the Price System*. The sudden vogue of technocracy in 1932 led to the reissue of the book, and for a while it became a best seller, with an average sale of 150 copies a week. In recent years, the rapid expansion of the technical class of employees (in 1900, there was one engineer for every 225 factory workers; in 1950, one for every 62; and in 1960, one for every 20), the rise of computer technology and automation, the engineering exploration of space, and the new prestige of the scientist have all focused attention on the strategic importance of the technologists, and these speculations recall the excitement that greeted Veblen's book when it was first published as a series of essays in 1919 in *The Dial* and then published in 1921 as a book.

The reasons for this excitement are not hard to find. *The Engineers and the Price System* is one of Veblen's few prophetic books. The tantalizing "Memorandum on a Practicable Soviet of Technicians," the concluding essay, is *not*, as the blurb writer proclaimed on the jacket of the 1932 reissued volume, "to the engineers what the Communist Manifesto purported to be for the proletariat," for Veblen opens and closes that chapter with the ironic statement that "under existing circumstances there need be no fear, and no hope of an effectual revolutionary overturn in America" that could "flutter the sensibilities" of the Guardians of the Vested Interests. But the context of the book does seek to establish a drift of history and an agenda for the future.

[2]

Revolutions in the eighteenth century [Veblen wrote] were military and political; and the Elder Statesmen who now believe themselves to be making history still believe that revolutions can be made and unmade by the same ways and means in the twentieth century. But any substantial or effectual overturn in the twentieth century will necessarily be an industrial overturn; and by the same token, any twentieth century revolution can be combatted or neutralized only by industrial ways and means.

In this respect, *The Engineers and the Price System* is squarely in the center of the preoccupation that has attended the rise of sociology since its beginnings in the nineteenth century: namely, the scanning of the historical skies for portents of "the new class" which will overturn the existing social order. Henri de Saint-Simon, the master of Auguste Comte and one of the fathers of modern sociology, initiated this quest in 1816, when he began publishing an irregular periodical, *L'Industrie* (though he did not actually coin it, he popularized the term *industrialism*), which sought to describe the society of the future. Past society, Saint-Simon said, had been military society, in which the chief figures were priests, warriors, and feudal lords—"the parasites" and consumers of wealth. The new industrial society, he said, would be ruled by the producers—the engineers and the entrepreneurs, the "coming men" of the times.[1] Karl Marx, of course, made the confrontation of capitalist and worker the central figure of his drama of modern history, but already in his time, some of Marx's opponents, such as Mikhail Bakunin and Alexander Herzen, were warning the workers that the victory of socialism would lead not to a classless society but to the emergence of a new class, the intellectuals

[1] For a more intensive discussion, see Frank E. Manuel, *The New World of Henri Saint-Simon* (Cambridge: Harvard University Press, 1956), especially Chapter 16, and *Selected Writings of Henri Comte de Saint-Simon,* edited by F. M. H. Markham (Oxford: Basil Blackwell, 1952).

ruling in the name of the workers.[2] The identity of this new class has been central to the elitist sociology of Mosca, Michels, and Pareto. James Burnham achieved a flash of notoriety in the early 1940's with his theme (a vulgarization of the work of two European syndicalists, Waclaw Machajski and Bruno Rizzi) of "the managerial revolution" as the coming stage of collectivist society. In American sociology, Harold Lasswell has written (most notably in his *World Politics and Personal Insecurity*) of the "skill groups" that must inevitably dominate any future society.

And in this regard Veblen, too, must be ranked on the side of the elitists. *If* a revolution were to come about in the United States—as a practiced skeptic, he was highly dubious of that prospect—it would not be led by a minority political party, as in Soviet Russia, which was a loose-knit and backward industrial region, nor would it come from the trade-union "votaries of the dinner pail," who, as a vested interest themselves, simply sought to keep prices up and labor supply down. It would occur, he said, along the lines "already laid down by the material conditions of its productive industry." And, turning this Marxist prism to his own perceptions, Veblen continued: "These main lines of revolutionary strategy are lines of technical organization and industrial management; essentially lines of industrial engineering; such as will fit the organization to take care of the highly technical industrial system that constitutes the indispensable material foundation of any modern civilized community."

The heart of Veblen's assessment of the revolutionary class is thus summed up in his identification of the "production engineers" as the indispensable "General Staff of the industrial system."

Without their immediate and unremitting guidance and correction the industrial system will not work. It is a mechanically

[2] For a summary of these concerns, see Max Nomad, *Aspects of Revolt* (New York: Bookman Associates, 1959).

organized structure of the technical processes designed, installed and conducted by the production engineers. Without them and their constant attention the industrial equipment, the mechanical appliances of industry, will foot up to just so much junk.

Thus the intellectual commitment was made: "The chances of anything like a Soviet in America, therefore, are the chances of a Soviet of technicians . . ." although, as was his wont, Veblen immediately backs off by remarking that "anything like a Soviet of Technicians is at the most a remote contingency in America." Given his style of exaggerated circumlocution and deliberate indirection, this is, at best, what we can pin Veblen down to saying: *If* a revolution ever could come about in the United States, a revolution that would break the power of the vested interests, it would come from the engineers, who have a true motive for revolution—since the requirements of profit-making must traduce their calling—and who have the strategic position and the means to carry through a revolution.

In a curious way, all of this represented a radical departure for Veblen. Before 1919 he had paid little attention to the engineers, though one of the persistent themes of his major work, *The Theory of Business Enterprise*, is the inherent conflict between "business," the financial interests who are concerned primarily with profit, and "industry," those forces which are geared to production. His fundamental concept, the idea of the "machine process," implied that because of the rationality of the machine a new race of men was being bred who replaced rule-of-thumb methods or intuitive skills with reasoned procedures based on the discipline of science. Yet he had never before tied these themes to the engineer. Typically, Veblen always left his concepts magnificently abstract, or he skillfully played the game of personification (e.g., "the captains of industry"), in which the social role rather than the person was manifest. Now, in 1919, Veblen seemingly made a basic sociological commitment—the identification of a concrete social group as the force that could, and possibly would, reshape society.

The postwar period was a critical one in Veblen's life, and the books he wrote at this time, *The Vested Interests and the State of the Industrial Arts* and *The Engineers and the Price System*, bear a somewhat different relation to his purposes than does the rest of his work. It would be too much to say that Veblen in this period had hopes of becoming a revolutionary leader; this was out of keeping with his dour personality and the heavy personal armor with which he kept most of the world, and even his friends, at a distance. But it does seem to be the case that at this time Veblen suddenly felt that he might become a prophet (he had always been an oracle, and his writings were suitably Delphic) who would rouse the latent forces of change in America. And among these forces—or so he was led to believe by some of his disciples—were the engineers.

THE ACADEMIC FLOATER

In 1919, at the age of sixty-two, Veblen had begun a new life, although two years earlier it had seemed that his career was at an end.[3] Less than twenty years before, he had

---

[3] In this section, and the next few, I have drawn largely on Joseph Dorfman's fine biography of Veblen, *Thorstein Veblen and His America* (New York: Viking Press, 1934), and, in particular, on two unpublished doctoral theses, Samuel Haber's "Scientific Management and the Progressive Movement" (Berkeley: University of California, 1961) and Edwin T. Layton's "The American Engineering Profession and the Idea of Social Responsibility" (Los Angeles: University of California, 1956). In addition, I have profited considerably from Mr. Layton's article "Veblen and the Engineers," in the *American Quarterly*, XIV (Spring 1962), although I think he overstates Veblen's confusions of the distinctions between different types of engineers. Additional sources were the article "Veblen *and* Technocracy," by Leon Ardzrooni, in *Living Age* (March 1933); *Scientific Management and the Unions*, by Milton Nadworny (Cambridge: Harvard

written his first book, *The Theory of the Leisure Class* (having had to guarantee almost all the costs of publication himself), and this book, largely through the efforts of William Dean Howells, had gained him widespread attention. His second book, *The Theory of Business Enterprise,* published in 1904, won him the even more intense admiration of an eager group of young economists. But "professionally" this farm-boy son of Norwegian immigrants was a "failure."

Throughout his life, Veblen was unable to find a permanent niche in the academic hierarchy. Although he had completed his Ph. D. at Yale at the age of twenty-seven (itself a remarkable achievement, considering the fact that he spoke almost no English until he entered the preparatory division of Carleton College, when he was seventeen), Veblen did not get his first academic job until he was thirty-five, when J. Lawrence Laughlin, with whom he had studied economics at Cornell, took him along to the nascent University of Chicago as a Fellow. Veblen stayed at the University of Chicago for fourteen years, but the administration regarded him with a cold eye (as much for his amatory difficulties as for his economic heresies), and he never rose higher than an assistant professorship, despite his publishing the aforementioned books, editing the *Journal of Political Economy*, and writing half a dozen major essays, including those on Karl Marx and socialist economics, reprinted in *The Place of Science in Modern Civilization.*

In 1906, Veblen was offered a post as associate professor of economics at Stanford University by David Starr Jordan, who was trying to strengthen the school's academic reputation. For the first time, Veblen had an opportunity to move up the academic ladder, but his stay at Stanford

University Press, 1955); the biography of Morris L. Cooke, *The Life and Times of a Happy Liberal,* by Kenneth Trombley (New York: Harper & Brothers, 1954); and David Riesman's provocative psychoanalytic interpretation, *Thorstein Veblen* (New York: Charles Scribner's Sons, 1953).

University was dismal. Veblen was indifferent about his courses and uninterested in his students, and, to cap it all, he got involved in an adulterous episode that became a campus scandal. In December of 1909 he was forced to resign his post.[4] For a year Veblen was unable to find another job, and then, through the intervention of a former student, H. J. Davenport, he was invited to the University of Missouri as a lecturer.

For seven years Veblen suffered the small-town oppressiveness of Columbia, Missouri. He tried desperately to leave, going so far as to apply to the Library of Congress for a routine bibliographical position—he was turned down as being too bright for the job. During the dispirited years at Missouri, Veblen's output slackened. He wrote *The Instinct of Workmanship*, an uneven book that reflects more sharply than any of his others the evolutionary anthropology that guided his viewpoint, and (after a summer in Europe in 1914) *Imperial Germany and the Industrial Revolution*, a brilliant account of the way German feudal culture had grafted a highly advanced technology on the society in order to promote dynastic ends.

In 1917, by "mutual consent," Veblen took a leave of absence from the University of Missouri to go to Washington; he never returned to formal academic life. A year later he celebrated his departure by publishing *The Higher Learning in America*, whose subtitle, "A Memorandum on the Conduct of the Universities by Businessmen," only hints at its savage indictment of higher education. (The manuscript, written a few years before he left Missouri, had been withheld from publication at the suggestion of the University's president; its original subtitle had been "A Study in Total Depravity.")

---

[4] For a sad but charming account of Veblen at this time, see a memoir by R. L. Duffus, *The Innocents at Cedro: A Memoir of Thorstein Veblen and Some Others* (New York: Macmillan Company, 1944).

The war itself engaged all of Veblen's attention and energy. His stay in Germany and his tolerance of Woodrow Wilson (not his faith in Wilson, since Veblen was incapable of any such commitment) led him to support the Allied cause. He believed, moreover, that the war not only would demonstrate the requirements of rational planning, because of the need to mobilize total capacity, but would allow the victorious Allied nations to make an attempt at social reconstruction. In 1916, working at feverish speed, Veblen had written *An Inquiry into the Nature of Peace and the Terms of Its Perpetuation* (published largely at his own expense), which expounded these ideas. Making a distinction between democratic and dynastic governments, Veblen noted that in the latter the survival of "barbarian" impulses made them consistently more aggressive and warlike; "perpetual peace," he concluded, could be maintained not only by finally disposing of all monarchic regimes, but by eliminating everywhere "the price-system and its attendant business enterprise" —Veblen's euphemism for capitalism.

The book came out at a propitious psychological moment. By the spring of 1917, when *The Nature of the Peace* was published, virtually the entire intelligentsia of the progressive movement (Herbert Croly, Walter Lippmann, John Dewey) as well as the intellectual leaders of the Socialist party (William English Walling, John Spargo, A. M. Simons, Jack London, Upton Sinclair) were supporting America's entry into the war and repudiating their earlier anti-war stands.[5] *The Nature of the Peace* allowed the intelligentsia both to justify their attitude against German militarism and to hope for the emergence of a new rational society after the war. The book was an immediate success, and was praised in all the liberal magazines. Francis Hackett, an

---

[5] For a discussion of this episode, see my monograph, "The Background and Development of Marxian Socialism in the United States," in *Socialism and American Life* (Princeton: Princeton University Press, 1952), pp. 312 passim.

editor of the *New Republic*, which was the organ of the progressive intelligentsia, called it "the most momentous work in English on the encompassment of lasting peace," and the Carnegie Endowment for International Peace purchased five hundred copies for distribution in colleges and universities. Veblen quickly became an international figure, and letters were written to him from all parts of the world. "Now," he said, "they are beginning to pay some attention to me."

It was in this mood that, in October 1917, Veblen went to Washington. As his biographer, Joseph Dorfman, remarks, "He wanted to be at the centre of things, and he hoped that he could be made use of on the paramount questions of the plans for peace." He saw Newton D. Baker, the Secretary of War, and Supreme Court Justice Louis D. Brandeis, but no one in a high position was interested in Veblen's ideas. He was invited to submit some memoranda to a group (whose secretary was Walter Lippmann, then of the *New Republic*) that had been set up by Wilson's confidant, Colonel Edward M. House, to prepare material on the terms of a possible peace settlement. One of Veblen's two memoranda discussed the problem of creating a "League of Pacific Peoples"; the other, on the "Economic Penetration of Backward Countries and of Foreign Investments," proposed the regulation of investment by the "Pacific League." Both were duly filed, but Veblen, discouraged, took a job with the statistical division of the Food Administration, where, with the aid of Isadore Lubin, he prepared a study of price control on foodstuffs.

Meanwhile Veblen's books, with their cool, sardonic tone, were getting its author into trouble. Although the Committee on Information, an official propaganda agency, praised his *Imperial Germany*, the Post Office Department, which was in charge of censorship, declared the book nonmailable under the Espionage Act. The American Defense Society and other jingoist groups complained to the Department of Justice about Veblen's attitude in *The Nature of the Peace* and *Imperial Germany* (complained, that is, about its mocking treatment of the democracies).

The book was read by an agent of the department who, although he could not understand Veblen's vocabulary, found the programme for the punishing of Germany so far ahead of anything that had been proposed by the entente, that he concluded that Veblen was a superpatriot, and refused to pay any attention to the complaints.[6]

The University of Missouri was behind him, his fruitless work with the Food Administration had ended, and Veblen was again without a job. Negotiations with Cornell University came to nothing. Two of his former students, Walton Hamilton and Walter Stewart, arranged for Veblen to give a series of lectures at Amherst in May 1918, and shortly afterward Jett Lauck, another former student, who was executive secretary of the War Labor Board, offered Veblen a job with the board as an examiner, at $4,800 a year—ironically, higher than any academic salary he had ever received. Veblen at first agreed to take the job, but when through the intervention of Horace Kallen he was invited to join the editorial board of *The Dial*, he gladly accepted. *The Dial* was to be the occasion of a short but significant new phase in his life.

POSTWAR DISILLUSIONMENT

In June 1918, Veblen moved to New York and joined *The Dial*. The magazine had an old and honorable name in American letters. The first *Dial* had been founded by Ralph Waldo Emerson and Margaret Fuller, in 1840, and was the parent of all the hundreds of little magazines that followed. Like many of its progeny, the original *Dial* had a short but

---

[6] Dorfman, *Thorstein Veblen and His America*, p. 382.

brilliant life. Failing to gain more than three-hundred sub-scribers, it suspended publication in 1844. In 1880, a Chicago publisher revived the name and continued to publish it as a sedate fortnightly review; in 1916 it was reorganized by Martyn Johnson as a literary journal with a staff consisting of Conrad Aiken, Randolphe Bourne, Padraic Colum and Van Wyck Brooks.[7] Two years later, under the influence of one of its owners, Helen Marot, a liberal woman who had written *American Labor Unions, by a Member, Helen Marot,* the magazine announced its removal to New York and a broadening of its scope to include "internationalism and a program of reconstruction in industry and education." The editors were to be John Dewey, Thorstein Veblen, Helen Marot, and George Donlin,[8] and the magazine set out to compete directly with the *Nation* and the *New Republic.* Veblen, clearly, was its star.

His experiences in Washington had left him bitter and resentful. The extraordinary thing was that he had lived his entire life, if not in an ivory tower, at least in its academic banlieus; and his protective tone of irony, his superior gamesmanship in the mimetic combat of pedantry, had not really prepared him to operate in the bureaucratic labyrinths of power. As David Riesman remarks:

In all this, Veblen appears to have been somewhat naive to assume that an elderly professor, inexperienced in practical affairs, would be eagerly welcomed, even by sympathizers in office. He expected miracles from the War itself—and possibly also as a result of his own willingness to come out, at long last, from behind his shell.[9]

[7] For a history of the successive changes in the makeup of *The Dial,* see Frederick J. Hoffman, Charles Allen, and Carolyn Ulrich, *The Little Magazine: A History and Bibliography* (Princeton: Princeton University Press, 1946), p. 7, and pp. 196-208.

[8] The associate editors were Clarence Britten, Harold Stearns, Randolph Bourne, and Scofield Thayer.

[9] Riesman, *Thorstein Veblen,* p. 31.

A woman spurned in love turns to reform as a second choice; a man scorned by power often turns to revolution. Veblen had always been subversive in his verbal irony; now, in the next two years, from 1919 to 1921, he began to entertain hopes, always somewhat masked, of becoming an active political force. A sense of revolutionary excitement was in the air and Veblen responded to it strongly. Writing as a journalist for the general public, he slashed out, more overtly than he ever had before, at the "vested interests" and their control of industry. He became intensely interested in the Russian Revolution (though he was never active in the "worker's soviet" formed at *The Dial* in the summer of 1919!); and in an article in *The Dial,* "Bolshevism Is a Menace—to Whom?" Veblen interpreted Bolshevism simply as the carrying of the principle of democracy into industry, or as just another name for the industrial republic.

More than that, Veblen was becoming popular, even something of a fad. *The Theory of the Leisure Class* had been reissued; it was approved by *Vanity Fair*, the magazine of the sophisticates, and had become required reading in intellectual circles.[10] The essays in *The Dial* were widely read, although an old friend of Veblen's, Walton Hamilton,

---

[10] "In 1919, Mencken wrote an essay on Veblen, in the magazine, *Smart Set,* which was later republished in his first *Prejudices.* Until 1917, said Mencken, Professor Dewey was the great thinker in the eyes of the respectable literary weeklies, a role he had fallen into after the death of William James. 'Then, overnight, the upspringing of the intellectual soviets, the headlong assault upon the old axioms of pedagogical speculation, the nihilistic dethronement of Professor Dewey—and rah, rah, rah for Prof. Dr. Thorstein Veblen!'

" 'In a few months—almost it seemed a few days—he was all over *The Nation, The Dial, The New Republic* and the rest of them, and his bookstand pamphlets began to pour from the presses, and newspapers reported his every wink and whisper,' and 'everyone of intellectual pretensions read his works. Veblenianism was shining in full brilliance. There were Veblenists, Veblen clubs, Veblen remedies, for all the sorrows of the world. There were even in Chicago, Veblen Girls—perhaps Gibson Girls grown middle-aged and despairing.' " Dorfman, *Thorstein Veblen and His America,* p. 423.

felt that as a journalist Veblen the agitator and phrase-maker was taking precedence over the thinker. Reviewing in the *New Republic* the first group of essays, published in book form as *The Vested Interests*, Hamilton remarked that even though readers would take over the phrases—in many cases they were quite imponderable when analyzed—sympathizers would get more "psychic income than intellectual ammunition from the volume."

But Veblen's savage mood reflected accurately the combination of postwar disillusionment, revolutionary anger, nihilism, and dadaism that was dominating the intellectual circles, and he, in turn, responded to these currents.[11]

It was during this period, too, that Veblen wrote one of his most incisive essays, "The Intellectual Pre-Eminence of Jews in Modern Europe" (in the *Political Science Quarterly* of March 1919),[12] which is at the same time a revealing self-portrait of the Norwegian farm boy who had left his own hermetic culture. The intellectually gifted Jew, he wrote, like other men in a similar position, secures immunity from intellectual quietism

at the cost of losing his secure place in the scheme of conventions into which he has been born, and . . . of finding no similarly secure place in the scheme of gentile conventions into which he is thrown. . . . He becomes a disturber of the intellectual peace, but only at the cost of becoming an intellectual wayfaring man, a wanderer in the intellectual No Man's Land, seeking another place to rest, farther along the road, somewhere over the

---

[11] "The hero of Ben Hecht's novels is a disgusted young man; everywhere he sees people and institutions designed to trap him, to cut him down to their size. He is a 'philosopher' fond of commenting upon the dreary stupidity of his inferiors and of quoting the 'best authorities' he has read. The authorities he knows best are Nietzsche and Veblen, though he also remembers the titles of many books." Frederick J. Hoffman, *The Twenties: American Writing in the Postwar Decade* (New York: Viking Press, 1955), p. 93.

[12] Reprinted in *Essays on Our Changing Order,* edited by Leon Ardzrooni (New York: Viking Press, 1934).

horizon. They are neither a complaisant nor a contented lot, these aliens of the uneasy feet.

In April 1919, Veblen began a new series in *The Dial,* on "Contemporary Problems in Reconstruction," which, according to an announcement in the magazine, was intended to be "a concrete application of [Veblen's] theory, outlined in *The Modern Point of View and the New Order.*" [13] These essays, later brought out in book form, became *The Engineers and the Price System.*

The heart of the book is in the last three essays. The first three sketch themes Veblen had already discussed in previous writings, although at this point he singled out the investment banker rather than the corporation head as the dominant figure in economic life ("regulating the rate and volume of output" in industrial enterprises under his control); and the old corporation financier is no longer a captain of industry but a lieutenant of finance. Specifically the last three essays, beginning with the chapter "On the Danger of a Revolutionary Overturn," represent a political departure from his earlier work.

These essays were written at the height of the "red scare," the drum-fire campaign initiated by Attorney General A. Mitchell Palmer, which included wholesale roundups of suspected radicals, raids on various radical meetings (including the breakup of the underground convention of the nascent Communist party in Bridgman, Michigan), and the deportation of anarchists. Against the same threat of revolution, about twenty states began passing criminal syndicalist laws, which made advocacy, rather than acts, of violence a crime.

Veblen's essays, as Dorfman has noted, were "conspicuous for their recklessness and their savage use of in-

[13] That is, the essays published from October 19, 1918, to January 25, 1919, and published in book form under the title of *The Vested Interests and the State of the Industrial Arts.*

verted meaning." Bolshevism, Veblen says, is the danger that

"the Vested Interests are facing," and "the Elder Statesmen are . . . in a position to know, without much inquiry, that there is no single spot or corner in civilized Europe, or America, where the underlying population would have anything to lose by such an overturn of the established order as would cancel the vested rights of privilege and property, whose guardian they are."

Some observers, continued Veblen, foresee a revolutionary overturn in two years; others, less intimately acquainted with the facts, predict a later date. Veblen, tongue in cheek, constantly reiterates that the Guardians of the Vested Interests have nothing to fear, but in each case the statement carries the sly addition "just yet." It is in this context that Veblen began to write of the engineers in words which seemed to say, "And now, I hear the tocsin of revolution, and it cannot be far away."

Hitherto these men, who so make up the general staff of the industrial system, have not drawn together into anything like a self-directing working force [he writes. *But*] Right lately these technologists have begun to become uneasily "class-conscious" and to reflect that they together constitute the indispensable General Staff of the industrial system. Their class consciousness has taken the immediate form of a growing sense of waste and confusion in the management of industry by the financial agents of the absentee owners. . . . So the engineers are beginning to draw together and ask themselves, "What about it?"

In all this, Veblen's mode of calculated ambiguity and abstracted specification heightens the tension, building up hints of an extraordinary ground swell among the engineers. But no persons are ever identified, no groups are ever named. In pointing to the sources of unrest, Veblen refers generally to "the consulting engineer" and "the management expert" who, in appraising the efficiency of business enterprises for the investment banker, have come to understand the "pervading lag, lack and friction" in the industrial system; and to the "younger generation," trained in the "stubborn logic of technology," who are "beginning to draw together on a common ground of understanding."

And yet it was Veblen, and not the Guardians of the Vested Interests, who was deceived. The movement that he thought was a "class-conscious effort" by engineers to end the "all-pervading mismanagement of industry" was, in its most immediate organizational thrust, an attempt to give engineers a distinct "professional" status in society. In its extremely vague import, it was a chimerical "technocratic eudaemonism" which resembled, if it resembled anything at all, Plato's *Republic*, but ruled by the engineer rather than the philosopher.

The "movement," if it can even be characterized by that term, was largely the work of two men, Morris L. Cooke and Henry Gantt. And, such is the comedy of the thing, it represented not a revolutionary dissenting group, but an effort by messianic disciples of Frederick W. Taylor, the "father" of scientific management, to extend Taylor's ideas, as they understood them, to American society at large.

THE GOSPEL OF EFFICIENCY

Frederick W. Taylor, a fascinating, if nowadays neglected, figure was indisputably the shaper of "modern" capitalism. If any social upheaval can ever be attributed to a single person, the logic of efficiency as the rule of contemporary life is due to him. For what he did was to establish the principle and methods for the rationalization of work.

But Taylor was more than an engineer. In his own mind's eye, he was a prophet who felt that he had discovered the "scientific principles" that would settle all social conflicts.[14]

This *éclaircissement* began when Taylor in 1882, then working as a mechanical engineer at the Midvale Steel Company in Philadelphia, became discouraged by the fact that the workmen he directed refused to work as fast as he thought they should. The solution, he felt, lay in the fact that no one knew what constituted a "fair day's work," and one reason was that not even management had any notion of a man's capacity, the fatigue a specific job engendered, the pace at which a man should work, the number of pieces that could be turned out in a specified period of time, or the speed at which any particular set of operations should take place. Out of Taylor's reflections (and his own compulsive character) came the idea of scientific time study and, more broadly, the measurement of work—for it is with the measurement of work and the idea of unit costs, rather than with the introduction of the factory as such, that modern industry gains distinctive meaning as a new way of life—and, following this, the practice of scientific management.

Taylor's principles were based upon the following: the time it takes to do a specific job; incentives and bonus systems for exceeding norms; differential rates of pay based on job evaluation; the standardization of tools and equipment; the fitting of men to jobs on the basis of physical and mental tests; and the removal of all planning and scheduling from the work floor itself into a new planning and scheduling department, a new superstructure, the responsibility for which was in the hands of the engineer. By setting "scientific" standards, Taylor felt that he could specify the "one best way" or the "natural laws" of work, and so remove the

---

[14] For a discussion of Taylor and his influence, see my essay, "Work and Its Discontents," in *The End of Ideology* (Illinois: Free Press of Glencoe, 1960).

basic source of antagonism between worker and employer—what is "fair" or "unfair." [15]

Morris L. Cooke, one of the two men Veblen had in mind when he spoke of the "uneasy . . . sense of waste and confusion" felt by the "General Staff of the industrial system," was a Philadelphia-born mechanical engineer who, while working in a number of shipyards before the turn of the century, was "sickened by the heartlessness on the part of the employers" and the "inefficiency on the part of the workers." [16] Discovering the work of Frederick W. Taylor while he was in this mood, Cooke responded like a religious convert.

To Cooke, and to many other young engineers, Taylor's ideas were excitingly "progressive," and the standpat resistance of turn-of-the-century industry to these innovations only reinforced their fervor. Moreover, Cooke and the others felt that such a conception of the engineer gave him a new professional status and that crucial recognition which hitherto he had been denied. Even further, Cooke was lured, as were other engineers, by Taylor's gospel declaration that "the same principles [of scientific management] can be applied with equal force to all social activities: to the management of our homes; the management of our farms; the management of the business of our tradesmen large and small; of our churches, our philanthropic institutions, our universities, and our governmental departments." [17] In effect, the engineer was to be the hierophant of the new society.

About 1910, when Taylor's ideas were beginning to catch on rapidly, hundreds of persons proclaimed themselves "efficiency engineers," promising to install his "system" in half the two to four years' time Taylor had felt necessary

---

[15] See Frederick W. Taylor, *The Principles of Scientific Management,* p. 10, reprinted in the compendium *Scientific Management* (New York: Harper & Brothers, 1947).

[16] Trombley, *The Life and Times of a Happy Liberal,* p. 8.

[17] See Taylor, *Principles of Scientific Management,* p. 8.

for the conversion of a plant. The prophet of scientific management openly announced that only four engineers were authorized to teach his theories. "They were men who had worked with him intimately and knew his every thought and wish." These four were C. G. Barth, H. K. Hathaway, Morris L. Cooke, and Henry L. Gantt. "Taylor let it be known that these four only had his blessing and that all others were operating on their own." [18]

Henry L. Gantt had been Taylor's chief assistant in the early experiments at the Midvale Steel Plant and later at the Bethlehem Steel Company. Later, he became an independent consulting engineer, installing the Taylor system into many different factories and earning the enmity of the American Federation of Labor, which, in 1914, had opened a campaign against "scientific management." In 1916, a year after Taylor's death, Gantt became the spokesman of a new technocratic orientation. Under the influence of Veblen, whose works he had begun to read, and of Charles Ferguson, an engineer and "an eccentric social gospeller, who wanted to reform business in order to develop its spiritual potentialities," [19] Gantt founded an organization called the New Machine. Gantt attacked the incompetence of the "financiers" and argued that the community should not have to bear the costs of such inefficiency. He assumed that the business system was going to collapse, and that the ground had to be prepared for his successor. In one of his essays, Gantt declared, "We can no longer follow the lead of those who have

[18] Trombley, *Life and Times of a Happy Liberal,* p. 9. The proselytizing efforts of the Taylorites and the formation of the Taylor Society, the forerunner of the present Society for the Advancement of Management, is a fascinating study of the engineering and progressive mentalities, but far beyond the scope of this essay. For the best accounts of these efforts, see Milton J. Nadworny, *Scientific Management and the Unions,* and the unpublished doctoral thesis of Samuel Haber.

[19] I have relied upon Edwin Layton's doctoral thesis for this characterization of Gantt.

axes to grind, disregarding economic laws; but must accord leadership to him who knows what to do and how to do it for the benefit of the community. This man is the engineer." [20]

The New Machine, however, was never a formal organization. It held a few discussion meetings which brought together about thirty-five interested engineers, but its only official act was to send a letter, in February 1917, to President Wilson, arguing that the industrial system would grow "only through a progressive elimination of plutocracy and all other forms of arbitrary power." Most of the group was quickly involved in war work, including Gantt, who, working with the Ordnance Department, produced the famous Gantt Charts, a graphical analysis designed to permit quick and easy understanding of the state of production at any given time, and the New Machine lay dormant. Gantt, who never met Veblen, though he was friendly with Veblen's disciple, Leon Ardzrooni, was thus one of the chief sources of Veblen's idea of the impending revolutionary consciousness of the engineers.

Morris L. Cooke, whom Veblen did meet, was the other chief source, and it was Cooke's effort to reform the American Society for Mechanical Engineers that Veblen mistook for a new "class conscious" activity.[21] In 1905, when Frederick W. Taylor became president of the Society, he asked Cooke to conduct an analysis of its affairs and reorganize its procedures in accordance with the principles of scientific management. At this same time, Cooke began to realize that the Society was dominated by engineers employed by big business firms and the public utilities. In 1911, he became director of public works for the city of Philadelphia, as part of a reform administration. Seeking to ex-

[20] Nadworny, *Scientific Management and the Unions,* p. 107.

[21] I follow here largely the article by Edwin Layton in the *American Quarterly,* his unpublished doctoral thesis, and Trombley's biography of Cooke.

amine the electric rates charged the city by the private utilities, Cooke was outraged to discover that while these utilities were able to enlist the services of the most eminent members of the engineering profession, almost no prominent engineer was willing to act as a consultant for the city.

In 1915, Cooke was elected a vice-president of the A.S.M.E. and became the leader of a faction seeking to reform the organization. He attacked the Society's ties with the corporations, charging that the professional status of the engineers was being compromised by their subordination to big business. By 1919, Cooke had succeeded. The A.S.M.E. was reorganized to sever its ties with business and trade associations, and a new code of ethics was adopted, which stated that the first professional obligation of the engineer was to the standards of his profession, not to his employer. Thus, the ferment within the American Society of Mechanical Engineers, and some of Cooke's papers that led to the reorganization of the Society, provided another source for Veblen's memorandum about the "Soviet of Technicians."

Veblen had been introduced to the writings of Cooke and Gantt by a friend at Stanford University, Guido Marx, who was a professor of machine design. Cooke supplied Marx with copies of his papers, and probably of Gantt's as well; Marx, who had kept up a correspondence with Veblen, in turn sent them on to him. It seems clear that, in the heightened political excitement of the day, Veblen not only had some literary plans about the engineers, but that he— or his disciples—also nursed some vague expectations of actually inspiring a new movement that would look to him for prophetic leadership.

In the fall of 1919, Veblen left *The Dial,* which, in the course of reorganization, had become a literary magazine, and he joined the faculty of the newly founded New School for Social Research. The New School was an experiment in higher education. It set out to maintain postgraduate standards in the character of its courses, but to dispense with degrees, ceremonials, professional hierarchies, and other trappings of academe. It assembled a distinguished faculty, which, besides Veblen, included Charles A. Beard, James Harvey Robinson, Wesley Clair Mitchell (all of whom resigned from Columbia University), and some other distinguished American figures in the social sciences.

When the New School began to function, Veblen was writing his series of articles on the "Soviet of Technicians." As Dorfman puts it, "He had become obsessed with the important role of the technician, and felt that the New School provided the opportunity and headquarters for the group he planned." In October of that year, Veblen wrote to Guido Marx, stating that

"it is an intimate part of the ambitions of the New School to come into touch with the technical men who have to do with the country's industry, and know something about the state of things and the needs of industry." At the same time, he continued, "the younger generation among the technicians appear to be getting uneasy on their own account . . . and are loosely drawing together, and entering on an inquiry into the industrial conditions and speculating on a way out of the current muddle."

In sum, Veblen asked Marx to come to New York to give a course at the New School, and to help in the direction of an industrial inquiry. Actually, Veblen saw Marx as a potential leader of these "young engineers." The suggestion was made directly to Marx by Leon Ardzrooni, Veblen's amanuensis, who was on the faculty of the New School. In December, Ardzrooni wrote to Marx:

The situation is this: I have been hobnobbing with some of the members of the A.S.M.E. and find that they are very much upset about the present industrial muddle throughout the country. Some of them, with the connivance of certain prominent newspaper men, had nearly perfected plans to get together and discuss matters, under the guidance of H. L. Gantt. They are all convinced that there is something wrong somewhere, but they are still groping and need proper leadership. As you have probably heard, Gantt died quite recently, and, in speaking about the plans of these engineers, I told them we had in you the proper leader and, in case it was possible for you to come to New York, you could meet with them once a week, or oftener, and talk things over.[22]

Marx assumed that some large movement was under way, and modestly suggested that Morris Cooke would be the more logical person to replace Gantt as the leader of engineers, but Ardzrooni "preferred Marx, doubtlessly because he was already something of a convert to Veblenism." [23] Marx came to New York, and found, as he put it, that "no mature members of the A.S.M.E. appeared in the picture." A man named Howard Scott appeared proclaiming himself to be an engineer, but as Marx observed, "I could not believe he was a trained technician, his use of technical terms being highly inaccurate and his thought processes, to my mind, lacking in logical structure and being basically unrealistic." A conference was organized by Marx ("in line with what I thought would best fulfill Veblen's plans") bringing together some of the new leaders of the A.S M.E. (including Colonel Fred J. Miller, the president, and Cooke) and some of the New School faculty, but after a desultory session nothing further came of any proposed collaboration. Apparently Veblen continued to see Cooke, in particular to discuss a Giant Power Survey being undertaken by the engineers, but as Cooke remarked, "I must say that all my contacts with him were rather tenuous because he struck me as a man who was almost too frail for any kind of contacts. He was a bully good counsellor, but only as to theory. There was too little physique there to help on action." [24]

[22] Dorfman, *Thorstein Veblen and His America,* pp. 452-53.

[23] Layton, "Veblen and the Engineers," p. 69.

[24] Cited by Dorfman, *Veblen and His America,* p. 455. Curiously enough, the only biography of Cooke extant (written twenty years after Dorfman's biography of Veblen), by Kenneth E. Trombley, the

This seems to have been the sum total of all those dark hints about the emerging class-consciousness of the "indispensable General Staff of the industrial system." Marx returned to California; Howard Scott organized a pretentious Technical Alliance, with himself listed as chief engineer, and a temporary organizing committee which included such personages as the architect Frederick Ackerman, the electrical engineers Bassett Jones and Charles Steinmetz, and some younger economists (Leland Olds and Stuart Chase), as well as Veblen (though, as Ardzrooni noted in a letter to Marx, enclosing the prospectus, "I have learned that most men whose names . . . appear here [including Veblen] were never consulted or informed of any meeting.").

In February 1921, *The Engineers and the Price System* appeared in book form. The country was on its way back to normalcy. The American Society of Mechanical Engineers had settled down into its conservative groove. A similar reorganization had taken place in the American Institute of Mining Engineers, and its leader, Herbert Hoover, had become the national spokesman for all the insurgent engineers. (Cooke, who felt that Hoover was the "engineering method

---

editor of *The American Engineer,* though it is replete with references to Cooke's relations with Brandeis, Franklin D. Roosevelt, Frankfurter, David Lilienthal, Philip Murray, and dozens of others, contains no mention of Cooke's short tryst with Veblen. Since the "book was developed in the glow of the subject's irrepressible personality and soul-stirring inspiration," according to the author, Cooke's failure to talk about Veblen may be taken as evidence of the thinness of such a contact—from Cooke's point of view.

Layton, who worked through the Cooke papers (which included some exchanges between Cooke and Guido Marx), writes: "Marx contacted Cooke and arranged for him to give one of the lectures for the course at the New School. He also obtained from Cooke, a list of engineers who might be interested in the course and arranged a meeting between Veblen and Cooke. A meeting between the insurgent mechanical engineers and Veblen's group was held. But the engineers were unwilling to accept the leadership of Veblen and Marx. Cooke, though friendly, regarded them as spokesmen for the 'extreme left.'" "Veblen and the Engineers," pp. 69-70.

personified," had in 1919 endorsed Hoover for the Republican presidential nomination.) [25] There was little to indicate that a Soviet of technicians was in the offing. Curiously, though, Veblen let his words stand as written, with no editorial revision or foreword. And so it stands, a record of misunderstanding.

Veblen's remaining life was a sorry epilogue to these disappointed hopes of establishing his intellectual leadership in the country. In 1922, the New School was drastically overhauled and, of the "Big Four," Beard, Mitchell, and Robinson resigned. Veblen wanted to leave, but had nowhere to go. Efforts to find him a job in the city universities proved unsuccessful. His last major book, *Absentee Ownership*, was proving to be a grueling effort, and, as Dorfman writes, "he resorted more often than before to Roget's *Thesaurus*." The book, which picks up and elaborates more directly the arguments of *The Theory of Business Enterprise* of two decades before, was only indifferently received—the conservatives felt that the prevailing prosperity seemed to refute Veblen's argument, and the radicals were annoyed because Veblen had asserted that "the standard formalities of 'Socialism' and 'Anti-Socialism' are obsolete in the face of the new alignment of economic forces."

His appointment at the New School having come to an end, for the next few years Veblen lived on small stipends contributed by a former student and, for a while, on some "winnings" from a quixotic foray in the stock market. He

[25] "Veblen and the Engineers," p. 72. In assessing Hoover, as is the case with many other figures, there is always the danger of reading present-day images back into the past. Hoover, in 1919, because of his war-relief work, was widely regarded as a "progressive Republican" and was looked at askance by the conservative Republicans of the day. It is still relevant, though, that the highly touted "insurgency" of the engineers was actually an effort to "professionalize" their status, rather than to change the social order. For a contemporary evaluation of Hoover, which does remarkably well in reconstructing the mood of the wartime years and after, see Lewis L. Strauss, *Man and Decisions* (New York: Doubleday & Company, 1962), pp. 7-56.

neglected economic writing, and as "one of the things men do, when they grow old," he remarked, he turned back to the Norse tales and completed the translation of *The Laxdaela Saga*, which he had begun thirty-seven years before. After the death of his first wife, Ellen Rolfe, in 1926, Veblen returned to California to live at his absentee properties in Stanford. New investments proved a failure, and Veblen, anxious about money, was supported by the generosity of his friends. On August 3, 1929, he died of heart failure.

VEBLEN, THE UTOPIAN

The Engineers and the Price System is a "short course" in the Veblenian system, and it can serve as a simplified introduction to his ideas. Veblen always felt the need in all his writings to start from "first principles" (since these were so much at variance with classical economics), and so almost all his books after *The Theory of the Leisure Class* seem inordinately repetitious. But if they are read in sequence, one can discern a spiral in which themes set forth in earlier books are picked up and elaborated as the basis for further argument. Thus the opening chapter of *The Engineers and the Price System* begins with a tongue-in-cheek account of "sabotage," a word hitherto used to describe the tactics of the radical syndicalists, but which Veblen defines as the restriction of output practiced by business in order to maintain levels of profit. This thesis, already set forth in *The Theory of the Business Enterprise*, Veblen now ties in with the role of the investment banker, whom he regards, in his postwar analysis, as the key figure in the organization pooling system of the Federal Reserve; the investment banker becomes not only the stabilizer of the business system but also the figure who, in his effort to inflate values and restrict production, is responsible for business cycles and depressions. Thus the tension between nonutilized capacity and restriction becomes the central motif of the book and the basis for Veblen's conviction that if the engineer were to take over the direction of American society, there would be "the due allocation of resources and a consequent full and reasonably proportioned employment of the available equipment and manpower" of society.

There is much in *The Engineers and the Price System* that is surprisingly accurate and relevant to the present-day American economy. The 1958 Kefauver Committee reports on "administered prices" in the steel and auto industries read like a gloss of the opening chapter in Veblen's book.[26] His wry comments on "salesmanship," the argument that salesmanship is a substitute for price reduction ("It is the chief factor in the ever-increasing cost of living, which is in its turn the chief ground of prosperity among the business community. . . ."), still has a telling bite. And the discussion, in Chapter 2, of the cumulative "state of the industrial arts" as one of the chief contributions to progress (as against the older emphasis, in classical economics, on land, labor,

[26] We can best understand how such market control is exercised by examining the price-setting system, the so-called standard-volume concept employed by the auto industry. This system, which was developed by Donaldson Brown for General Motors in 1924, is based on an equation of three variables—price, net return on investment, and estimated average rate of plant operation. The price set for a single car is a function of the other two variables. But how are these determined? Net return on investment is simple: General Motors decides that it must get roughly a 20-per-cent return after taxes each year. "Estimated average rate of plant operation" is more complicated. Because of seasonal and other fluctuations in demand, General Motors estimates that in its *best* year it will utilize about 80 per cent of its maximum operating capacity. In an *average* year it figures on reaching 80 per cent of the production in its best year. Thus it figures, theoretically, on using 64 per cent of its capacity in any normal year. In actual practice, the "standard volume" has been calculated on a 55-per-cent capacity. In effect, therefore, General Motors so sets its prices as to plan for a return of 20 per cent a year on its investment on the assumption that its plants will operate through the year for a total of only 180 days, or 36 weeks. From 1950 to 1957, General Motors' actual sales were, on the average, about 30 per cent higher

and money capital as the co-ordinates of production) points up the increasing concern today with education, or "human capital," as the basic resource for technological and productive advance in society. The neglected point Veblen makes is that technology (the "state of the industrial arts") is a joint stock of knowledge derived from past experience—a social asset, which is no man's or no firm's individual property, though it is often claimed as such.

But his reiterated emphasis on technology also reveals the one-sidedness, or inadequacy, of the Veblenian system. He was indifferent to the social relations within the factory— both the elements that created bureaucracy and those that, as in the case of the engineers, made for insistence on professional status as one means of overcoming the impersonality that the rationalization of work imposes on modern life.[27] In his concentration on the machinations of credit, Veblen slighted the imaginative social invention that is the "fiction" of credit. If one looks at the nature of capital accumulation in a historical perspective, credit, a nineteenth-century device,

---

than the "standard volume" on which the company set its prices. Thus in 1950, General Motors estimated its "standard volume" at 2,250,000 units in order to give it a 20-per-cent return on investment, and sold 3,812,000 units, or a 69-per-cent "margin of safety."

The concept of "standard volume" is related to the idea of the "break-even point" (a measure that is based on the relationship between costs, both fixed and variable, and sales), or the figure at which a company begins to turn a profit. General Motors, in the 1950 decade, had a "break-even" point at about 48 per cent of sales; and if one took full capacity into account, the "break-even point" would come to between 40 and 45 per cent of capacity. In other words, General Motors could significantly reduce its prices, and still make enormous profits. As things stand, the "marginal firm" in the industry, Chrysler, holds up a neat "price umbrella" for General Motors.

For an elaboration of this data, and its consequences for the economy, see my article, "The Subversion of Collective Bargaining," in *Commentary,* March 1960.

[27] These are themes, of course, which are central to the writings of Weber and Durkheim, and which have been deeply evident in sociological writing in recent years.

is a "due bill" on the future, an expression of faith (necessarily based on political stability) in the growth of an economy; through such a lien on the future, one is able to employ resources that normally would have lain fallow. Credit thus becomes, as Schumpeter has pointed out, the basis for entrepreneurial activity.

Veblen's proposal to do away with the price system reveals a naïve notion of planning—akin to Marx's idea that the interest rate is merely an exploitative device, rather than an instrument to test the efficiency of capital, and has no place in a socialist economy. It is evident that direct physical planning of production (as in the experience of the American War Production Board during the Second World War, or the Soviet system of a "mobilized economy") can rapidly increase the output of a *few* final products—regardless of cost—to an astonishing extent. But it is also equally evident that any complex planning mechanism seeking to distribute resources efficiently (i.e., to assess relative costs) in the production of tens of thousands of *different* products can do so best, as even the socialist economies have discovered, only through a price system.

And, finally, the idea that revolution in the twentieth century can only be an "industrial overturn"—itself a syndicalist idea—underscores the "rationalist fallacy" that lies behind so much of Veblen's thought. No matter how increasingly technical the underlying social processes become—and in the advanced industrial countries, with the rise of computer technology and its consequent effect on the labor force, this process is rapid indeed—social change, at bottom, is a *political* decision; or rather, the crucial turning points in a society are ultimately determined not by crescive social changes, but only as these changes come to a head in some political form. Thus, in the case of the United States, the Veblenian analysis, because it is essentially *apolitical,* neglects the role of government, or of the federal budget, as the crucial determinant of economic growth and social power.

To generalize the concerns of a political sociology: in the advanced industrial, as well as in the newly industrializing, societies it is the military and political forces that remain the "movers and shakers" of change.

In all this—in his evolutionary schemes, his emphasis on the economics of production, his savage critiques of commerce and money (as well as in his neglect of other forces)—Veblen betrays his true intellectual lineage, one that his involuted style was successfully able to obscure.[28] This ancestry is not Marxist (in an effort to assert his own originality, one of the few forebears that Veblen attacks by name is Marx), but the utopian socialism of Fourier and Saint-Simon. The parallels with Fourier in Veblen's writing are astonishing. To show his contempt for the academic learning of his time, Fourier phrased the system he recapitulated endlessly in his various works in a set of neologisms that were deliberately meant to be incomprehensible to the laity. ("Fourier was conscious of the fact that he was pouring forth a torrent of newfangled words, and in his manuscripts he occasionally indulged in facetious self-mockery on this account. 'Hola, another neologism! Haro on the guilty one! but is this any worse than *doctrinaire?*' ")[29] Fourier's description of the

[28] "[Veblen's] usual failure to cite his sources in his writings would seem to have been due, to some extent, to a desire to seem original—a 'natural'—and to a slightly greater extent to a desire to evade another academic ritual, another debt, but, in addition, to some inner fear that a citation would act as a constraining force, limiting what he could say. Thus, for instance, if he should rest a particular statement about the handicraft era on Sombart's treatment of it, he would either have to put himself under obligation to Sombart's interpretation or to show why he departed from it, whereas by a rare, vague, and general reference he maintains his superiority to his sources. This practice, and many other elements in his make-up, led him to seek the doubtful security of abstraction—including an endlessly abstract and earnest call to other economists to be concrete. For abstraction allows one to glide over difficulties presented by individual instances. . . ." David Riesman, *Thorstein Veblen,* pp. 15-16.

[29] Frank E. Manuel, *The Prophets of Paris* (Cambridge: Harvard University Press, 1962), p. 201.

earlier stages of society as *savagery* and *barbarism* were taken up by Veblen in *The Theory of the Leisure Class*. And Fourier's indictment of capitalism—the *locus classicus* of such criticism, as Professor Manuel points out—concentrates on the thievery in the stock market, the "corruption of commerce," the miseries of economic crises, hoarding and speculation and the squandering of natural resources as all being endemic to the system.

Perhaps the most binding link between Veblen and the French Utopians is their two-fold view of society based on the pre-eminent virtue of production as the basic "good." For Fourier, as it was to be for Saint-Simon and, in his own way, for Veblen, those persons not directly connected with production—soldiers, bureaucrats, merchants, and lawyers— were parasites who lived at the expense of the producers.[30] (Veblen insisted that the elimination of salesmanship and all its voluminous apparatus and traffic would cut down the capitalized income of the business community by half.) And Saint-Simon, who constantly harped on the social waste, maladjustment, and friction produced in a nonrational society, felt that a "natural elite"—in his view, the men of science—would come to the fore in the inevitable development of the industrial order.[31]

The distinction between productive and unproductive labor, between industrial and pecuniary employments, runs as a peculiar thread through the writings of the Utopians, as it does through Veblen's,[32] and reflects at bottom the hatred —and fear—felt by the artisan mentality toward metropolitan life. What Veblen disliked about capitalism, as T. W. Adorno

[30] *The Prophets of Paris,* p. 217.

[31] Manuel, *The New World of Henri Saint-Simon,* pp. 303-04.

[32] The distinction between productive and unproductive labor exists in Adam Smith as in Marx, but in Smith, and to a grea... tent in Marx, the distinction is used analytically as a means of es... lishing a labor theory of value, whereas in the Utopians and in Veblen, the distinction becomes "ideological"—a stick for beating the enemy.

has shrewdly pointed out, was not its exploitation of the people but its waste of goods; and, like Frederick W. Taylor, he disliked every "superfluous" action. In the end, falling back on the "instinct of workmanship" as the basic virtue, Veblen the technocrat longed for the restoration of "the most ancient." It is the final irony, as Adorno indicates, "that in Veblen faith in Utopia necessarily takes the form which he so vigorously condemns in middle class society, the form of retrogression or 'reversion.' Hope, for him, lies solely with the primitive history of mankind. Every happiness barred to him because of the pressures of dreamless adjustment and adaptation to reality, to the conditions of the industrial world, shows him its image in some early golden age of mankind." [33]

Central to all this—to return to our earlier theme of the new class—is the elitist image, which was given its most mechanical shape in the doctrines of technocracy. Most of Veblen's admirers have sought to discredit the similarities [34] but the resemblance is clear, and while Veblen's doctrines

[33] T. W. Adorno, "Veblen's Attack on Culture," *Studies in Philosophy and Social Science*, IX (1941), 389-413.

[34] Though Leon Ardzrooni, Veblen's most faithful disciple, was quick to claim such credit in the winter of 1932, when the spreading vogue of technocracy led some of its followers to state that Howard Scott, the leader of the Technocratic movement, had inspired Veblen's thinking in *The Engineers and the Price System*. Ardzrooni wrote: "From this brief narrative it should be clear that Veblen had laid the foundations and worked out the details of what passes current as Technocracy and before his contact with Howard Scott." Ardzrooni then sketches the story of Veblen's (and his) efforts to provide leadership for the young engineers, though in his account ("Later on, at the earnest solicitation of Veblen and at some expense to the New School, a prominent and experienced engineer joined the group, chiefly for the purpose of consulting with Scott") the emphasis is put, surprisingly, and apparently for the purposes of establishing Veblen's originality, on consultation with Scott, rather than with the followers Gantt or with the Cooke groups in the American Society of Mechanical Engineers. See Leon Ardzrooni, "Veblen *and* Technocracy," *Living Age*, March 1933.

cannot be held accountable for the later phase of technocracy
—which flared again briefly in 1940 as a quasi-fascist movement, replete with gray uniforms and a monad symbol—the
"elective affinity" between Veblenianism and technocracy is
evident not only in the formal content of the ideas but in the
temperamental derivatives: the qualities of inhuman scientism
and formal rationalism, which in the end become an attack
upon culture itself.

The central feature of contemporary life is bureaucracy
—that vast cobweb of rules and procedures which lays down
"rational" grades or levels of accomplishments and orderly
prescriptions of conduct as the defined steps for rising or
finding a place in the world. It is an age of the specialist, the
expert, and the technician. Karl Marx, in his metaphysical
simplicity ("Man will be a hunter in the morning, a fisher-
man in the afternoon"), never envisaged that this would be
the fate of the socialist dream. Veblen, with his ironic military metaphors, had a more profound insight; for him the
technicians constituted the indispensable general staff of the
economic army, and one day, when the dawning consciousness of their power became clear to them, they would presumably take over as the rulers of the new society. That the
actual historical story—the literal contact with the engineers
—is a myth is less important than Veblen's need to envision
and proclaim such a myth as true.

In the coming decades, as any reading of changes in
our occupational structure indicates, we will be moving toward a "post-industrial society," in which the scientist, the
engineer, and the technician constitute the key functional
class in society. The question remains whether Veblen, in
envisaging such a change, which is the striking portent of
The Engineers and the Price System, finally abandoned the
cautions that had made him the "outsider" all his life, and

placed himself at the head of this wave of the future—saying, in effect, that the technological rule of society was good—or whether, in some final, mordant irony, in seeing such a society as the mechanized end-product of the "instinct of workmanship," he was playing a joke—and if so on whom?

COLUMBIA UNIVERSITY
SPRING 1963

I On the Nature and Uses of Sabotage

S*abotage" is a derivative of "sabot," which is French* for a wooden shoe. It means going slow, with a dragging, clumsy movement, such as that manner of footgear may be expected to bring on. So it has come to describe any manœuvre of slowing-down, inefficiency, bungling, obstruction. In American usage the word is very often taken to mean forcible obstruction, destructive tactics, industrial frightfulness, incendiarism and high explosives, although that is plainly not its first meaning nor its common meaning. Nor is that its ordinary meaning as the word is used among those who have advocated a recourse to sabotage as a means of enforcing an argument about wages or the conditions of work. The ordinary meaning of the word is better defined by an expression which has latterly come into use among the I. W. W., "conscientious withdrawal of efficiency"—although that phrase does not cover all that is rightly to be included under this technical term.

The sinister meaning which is often attached to the word in American usage, as denoting violence and disorder, appears to be due to the fact that the American usage has been shaped chiefly by persons and newspapers who have aimed to discredit the use of sabotage by organized workmen, and who have therefore laid stress on its less amiable manifestations. This is unfortunate. It lessens the usefulness of the word by making it a means of denunciation rather than of understanding. No doubt violent obstruction has had its share in the strategy of sabotage as carried on by disaffected workmen, as well as in the similar tactics of rival business concerns. It comes into the case as one method of sabotage, though by not means the most usual or the most effective; but it is so spectacular and shocking a method that it has drawn undue attention to itself. Yet such deliberate violence is, no doubt, a relatively minor fact in the case, as compared with that deliberate malingering, confusion, and misdirection of work that makes up the bulk of what the expert practitioners would recognize as legitimate sabotage.

The word first came into use among the organized French workmen, the members of certain *syndicats,* to describe their tactics of passive resistance, and it has continued to be associated with the strategy of these French workmen, who are known as syndicalists, and with their like-minded running-mates in other countries. But the tactics of these syndicalists, and their use of sabotage, do not differ, except in detail, from the tactics of other workmen elsewhere, or from the similar tactics of friction, obstruction, and delay habitually employed, from time to time, by both employees and employers to enforce an argument about wages and prices. Therefore, in the course of a quarter-century past, the word has quite unavoidably taken on a general meaning in common speech, and has been extended to cover all such peaceable or surreptitious manœuvres of delay, obstruction, friction, and defeat, whether employed by the workmen to enforce their claims, or by the employers to defeat their employees, or by competitive business concerns to get the better of their business rivals or to secure their own advantage.

Such manœuvres of restriction, delay, and hindrance have a large share in the ordinary conduct of business; but it is only lately that this ordinary line of business strategy has come to be recognized as being substantially of the same nature as the ordinary tactics of the syndicalists. So that it has not been usual until the last few years to speak of manœuvres of this kind as sabotage when they are employed by employers and their business concerns. But all this strategy of delay, restriction, hindrance, and defeat is manifestly of the same character, and should conveniently be called by the same name, whether it is carried on by business men or by workmen; so that it is no longer unusual now to find workmen speaking of "capitalistic sabotage" as freely as the employers and the newspapers speak of syndicalist sabotage. As the word is now used, and as it is properly used, it describes a certain system of industrial strategy or management, whether it is employed by one or another. What it describes is a resort to peaceable or surreptitious restriction, delay, withdrawal, or obstruction.

Sabotage commonly works within the law, although it may often be within the letter rather than the spirit of the law. It is used to secure some special advantage or preference, usually of a businesslike sort. It commonly has to do with something in the nature of a vested right, which one or another of the parties in the case aims to secure or defend, or to defeat or diminish; some preferential right or special advantage in respect of income or privilege, something in the way of a vested interest. Workmen have resorted to such measures to secure improved conditions of work, or increased wages, or shorter hours, or to maintain their habitual standards, to all of which they have claimed to have some sort of a vested right. Any strike is of the nature of sabotage, of course. Indeed, a strike is a typical species of sabotage. That strikes have not been spoken of as sabotage is due to the accidental fact that strikes were in use before this word came into use. So also, of course, a lockout is another typical species of sabotage. That the lockout is employed by the employers against the employees does not change the fact that it is a means of defending a vested right by delay, withdrawal, defeat, and obstruction of the work to be done. Lockouts have not usually been spoken of as sabotage, for the same reason that holds true in the case of strikes. All the while it has been recognized that strikes and lockouts are of identically the same character.

All this does not imply that there is anything discreditable or immoral about this habitual use of strikes and lockouts. They are part of the ordinary conduct of industry under the existing system, and necessarily so. So long as the system remains unchanged these measures are a necessary and legitimate part of it. By virtue of his ownership the owner-employer has a vested right to do as he will with his own property, to deal or not to deal with any person that offers, to withhold or withdraw any part or all of his industrial equipment and natural resources from active use for the time being, to run on half time or to shut down his plant and to lock out all those persons for whom he has no present use on his own premises. There is no question that the lockout is altogether a legitimate manœuvre. It may even be meritorious, and it is frequently considered to be meritorious when its use helps to maintain sound conditions in business—that is to say profitable conditions—as frequently happens. Such is the view of the substantial citizens. So also is the strike legitimate, so long as it keeps within the law; and it may at times even be meritorious, at least in the eyes of the strikers. It is to be admitted quite broadly that both of these typical species of sabotage are altogether fair and honest in principle, although it does not therefore follow that every strike or every lockout is necessarily fair and honest in its working-out. That is in some degree a question of special circumstances.

Sabotage, accordingly, is not to be condemned out of hand, simply as such. There are many measures of policy and management both in private business and in public administration which are unmistakably of the nature of sabotage and which are not only considered to be excusable, but are deliberately sanctioned by statute and common law and by the public conscience. Many such measures are quite of the essence of the case under the established system of law and order, price and business, and are faithfully believed to be indispensable to the common good. It should not be difficult to show that the common welfare in any community which is organized on the price system cannot be maintained without a salutary use of sabotage—that is to say, such habitual recourse to delay and obstruction of industry and such restriction of output as will maintain prices at a reasonably profitable level and so guard against business depression. Indeed, it is precisely considerations of this nature that are now engaging the best attention of officials and business men in their endeavors to tide over a threatening depression in American business and a consequent season of hardship for all those persons whose main dependence is free income from investments.

Without some salutary restraint in the way of sabotage on the productive use of the available industrial plant and workmen, it is altogether unlikely that prices could be maintained at a reasonably profitable figure for any appreciable time. A businesslike control of the rate and volume of output is indispensable for keeping up a profitable market, and a profitable market is the first and unremitting condition of prosperity in any community whose industry is owned and managed by business men. And the ways and means of this necessary control of the output of industry are always and necessarily something in the nature of sabotage—something in the way of retardation, restriction, withdrawal, unemployment of plant and workmen—whereby production is kept short of productive capacity.

The mechanical industry of the new order is inordinately productive. So the rate and volume of output have to be regulated with a view to what the traffic will bear—that is to say, what will yield the largest net return in terms of price to the business men who manage the country's industrial system. Otherwise there will be "overproduction," business depression, and consequent hard times all around. Overproduction means production in excess of what the market will carry off at a sufficiently profitable price. So it appears that the continued prosperity of the country from day to day hangs on a "conscientious withdrawal of efficiency" by the business men who control the country's industrial output. They control it all for their own use, of course, and their own use means always a profitable price.

In any community that is organized on the price system, with investment and business enterprise, habitual unemployment of the available industrial plant and workmen, in whole or in part, appears to be the indispensable condition without which tolerable conditions of life cannot be maintained. That is to say, in no such community can the industrial system be allowed to work at full capacity for any appreciable interval of time, on pain of business stagnation and consequent privation for all classes and conditions of men. The requirements of profitable business will not tolerate it. So the rate and volume of output must be adjusted to the needs of the market, not to the working capacity of the available resources, equipment and man power, nor to the community's need of consumable goods. Therefore there must always be a certain variable margin of unemployment of plant and man power. Rate and volume of output can, of course, not be adjusted by exceeding the productive capacity of the industrial system. So it has to be regulated by keeping short of maximum production by more or less as the condition of the market may require. It is always a question of more or less unemployment of plant and man power, and a shrewd moderation in the unemployment of these available resources, a "conscientious withdrawal of efficiency," therefore, is the beginning of wisdom in all sound workday business enterprise that has to do with industry.

All this is matter of course, and notorious. But it is not a topic on which one prefers to dwell. Writers and speakers who dilate on the meritorious exploits of the nation's business men will not commonly allude to this voluminous running administration of sabotage, this conscientious withdrawal of efficiency, that goes into their ordinary day's work. One prefers to dwell on those exceptional, sporadic, and spectacular episodes in business where business men have now and again successfully gone out of the safe and sane highway of conservative business enterprise that is hedged about with a conscientious withdrawal of efficiency, and have endeavored to regulate the output by increasing the productive capacity of the industrial system at one point or another.

But after all, such habitual recourse to peaceable or surreptitious measures of restraint, delay, and obstruction in the ordinary businesslike management of industry is too widely known and too well approved to call for much exposition or illustration. Yet, as one capital illustration of the scope and force of such businesslike withdrawal of efficiency, it may be in place to recall that all the civilized nations are just now undergoing an experiment in businesslike sabotage on an unexampled scale and carried out with unexampled effrontery. All these nations that have come through the war, whether as belligerents or as neutrals, have come into a state of more or less pronounced distress, due to a scarcity of the common necessaries of life; and this distress falls, of course, chiefly on the common sort, who have at the same time borne the chief burden of the war which has brought them to this state of distress.

The common man has won the war and lost his livelihood. This need not be said by way of praise or blame. As it stands it is, broadly, an objective statement of fact, which may need some slight qualification, such as broad statements of fact will commonly need. All these nations that have come through the war, and more particularly the common run of their populations, are very much in need of all sorts of supplies for daily use, both for immediate consumption and for productive use. So much so that the prevailing state of distress rises in many places to an altogether unwholesome pitch of privation, for want of the necessary food, clothing, shelter, and fuel. Yet in all these countries the staple industries are slowing down. There is an ever increasing withdrawal of efficiency. The industrial plant is increasingly running idle or half idle, running increasingly short of its productive capacity.

Workmen are being laid off and an increasing number of those workmen who have been serving in the armies are going idle for want of work, at the same time that the troops which are no longer needed in the service are being demobilized as slowly as popular sentiment will tolerate, apparently for fear that the number of unemployed workmen in the country may presently increase to such proportions as to bring on a catastrophe. And all the while all these peoples are in great need of all sorts of goods and services which these idle plants and idle workmen are fit to produce. But for reasons of business expediency it is impossible to let these idle plants and idle workmen go to work—that is to say for reasons of insufficient profit to the business men interested, or in other words, for the reasons of insufficient income to the vested interests which control the staple industries and so regulate the output of product. The traffic will not bear so large a production of goods as the community needs for current consumption, because it is considered doubtful whether so large a supply could be sold at prices that would yield a reasonable profit on the investment—or rather on the capitalization; that is to say, it is considered doubtful whether an increased production, such as to employ more workmen and supply the goods needed by the community, would result in an increased net aggregate income for the vested interests which control these industries. A reasonable profit always means, in effect, the largest obtainable profit.

All this is simple and obvious, and it should scarcely need explicit statement. It is for these business men to manage the country's industry, of course, and therefore to regulate the rate and volume of output; and also of course any regulation of the output by them will be made with a view to the needs of business; that is to say, with a view to the largest obtainable net profit, not with a view to the physical needs of these peoples who have come through the war and have made the world safe for the business of the vested interests. Should the business men in charge, by any chance aberration, stray from this straight and narrow path of business integrity, and allow the community's needs unduly to influence their management of the community's industry, they would presently find themselves discredited and would probably face insolvency. Their only salvation is a conscientious withdrawal of efficiency. All this lies in the nature of the case. It is the working of the price system, whose creatures and agents these business men are. Their case is rather pathetic, as indeed they admit quite volubly. They are not in a position to manage with a free hand, the reason being that they have in the past, under the routine requirements of the price system as it takes effect in corporation finance, taken on so large an overhead burden of fixed charges that any appreciable decrease in the net earnings of the business will bring any well-managed concern of this class face to face with bankruptcy.

At the present conjuncture, brought on by the war and its termination, the case stands somewhat in this typical shape. In the recent past earnings have been large; these large earnings (free income) have been capitalized; their capitalized value has been added to the corporate capital and covered with securities bearing a fixed income-charge; this income-charge, representing free income, has thereby become a liability on the earnings of the corporation; this liability cannot be met in case the concern's net aggregate earnings fall off in any degree; therefore prices must be kept up to such a figure as will bring the largest net aggregate return, and the only means of keeping up prices is a conscientious withdrawal of efficiency in these staple industries on which the community depends for a supply of the necessaries of life.

The business community has hopes of tiding things over by this means, but it is still a point in doubt whether the present unexampled large use of sabotage in the businesslike management of the staple industries will now suffice to bring the business community through this grave crisis without a disastrous shrinkage of its capitalization, and a consequent liquidation; but the point is not in doubt that the physical salvation of these peoples who have come through the war must in any case wait on the pecuniary salvation of these owners of corporate securities which represent free income. It is a sufficiently difficult passage. It appears that production must be curtailed in the staple industries, on pain of unprofitable prices. The case is not so desperate in those industries which have immediately to do with the production of superfluities; but even these, which depend chiefly on the custom of those kept classes to whom the free income goes, are not feeling altogether secure. For the good of business it is necessary to curtail production of the means of life, on pain of unprofitable prices, at the same time that the increasing need of all sorts of necessaries of life must be met in some passable fashion, on pain of such popular disturbances as will always come of popular distress when it passes the limit of tolerance.

Those wise business men who are charged with administering the salutary modicum of sabotage at this grave juncture may conceivably be faced with a dubious choice between a distasteful curtailment of the free income that goes to the vested interests, on the one hand, and an unmanageable onset of popular discontent on the other hand. And in either alternative lies disaster. Present indications would seem to say that their choice will fall out according to ancient habit, that they will be likely to hold fast by an undiminished free income for the vested interests at the possible cost of any popular discontent that may be in prospect—and then, with the help of the courts and the military arm, presently make reasonable terms with any popular discontent that may arise. In which event it should all occasion no surprise or resentment, inasmuch as it would be nothing unusual or irregular and would presumably be the most expeditious way of reaching a *modus vivendi*. During the past few weeks, too, quite an unusually large number of machine guns have been sold to industrial business concerns of the larger sort, here and there, at least so they say. Business enterprise being the palladium of the Republic, it is right to take any necessary measures for its safeguarding. Price is of the essence of the case, whereas livelihood is not.

The grave emergency that has arisen out of the war and its provisional conclusion is, after all, nothing exceptional except in magnitude and severity. In substance it is the same sort of thing that goes on continually but unobtrusively and as a matter of course in ordinary times of business as usual. It is only that the extremity of the case is calling attention to itself. At the same time it serves impressively to enforce the broad proposition that a conscientious withdrawal of efficiency is the beginning of wisdom in all established business enterprise that has to do with industrial production. But it has been found that this grave interest which the vested interests always have in a salutary retardation of industry at one point or another cannot well be left altogether to the haphazard and ill-coordinated efforts of individual business concerns, each taking care of its own particular line of sabotage within its own premises. The needed sabotage can best be administered on a comprehensive plan and by a central authority, since the country's industry is of the nature of a comprehensive interlocking system, whereas the business concerns which are called on to control the motions of this industrial system will necessarily work piecemeal, in severalty and at cross-purposes. In effect, their working at cross-purposes results in a sufficiently large aggregate retardation of industry, of course, but the resulting retardation is necessarily somewhat blindly apportioned and does not converge to a neat and perspicuous outcome. Even a reasonable amount of collusion among the interested business concerns will not by itself suffice to carry on that comprehensive moving equilibrium of sabotage that is required to preserve the business community from recurrent collapse or stagnation, or to bring the nation's traffic into line with the general needs of the vested interests.

Where the national government is charged with the general care of the country's business interests, as is invariably the case among the civilized nations, it follows from the nature of the case that the nation's lawgivers and administration will have some share in administering that necessary modicum of sabotage that must always go into the day's work of carrying on industry by business methods and for business purposes. The government is in a position to penalize excessive or unwholesome traffic. So, it is always considered necessary, or at least expedient, by all sound mercantilists, as by a tariff or by subsidies, to impose and maintain a certain balance or proportion among the several branches of industry and trade that go to make up the nation's industrial system. The purpose commonly urged for measures of this class is the fuller utilization of the nation's industrial resources in material, equipment, and man power; the invariable effect is a lowered efficiency and a wasteful use of these resources, together with an increase of international jealousy. But measures of that kind are thought to be expedient by the mercantilists for these purposes—that is to say, by the statesmen of these civilized nations, for the purposes of the vested interests. The chief and nearly the sole means of maintaining such a fabricated balance and proportion among the nation's industries is to obstruct the traffic at some critical point by prohibiting or penalizing any exuberant undesirables among these branches of industry. Disallowance, in whole or in part, is the usual and standard method.

The great standing illustration of sabotage administered by the government is the protective tariff, of course. It protects certain special interests by obstructing competition from beyond the frontier. This is the main use of a national boundary. The effect of the tariff is to keep the supply of goods down and thereby keep the price up, and so to bring reasonably satisfactory dividends to those special interests which deal in the protected articles of trade, at the cost of the underlying community. A protective tariff is a typical conspiracy in restraint of trade. It brings a relatively small, though absolutely large, run of free income to the special interests which benefit by it, at a relatively, and absolutely, large cost to the underlying community, and so it gives rise to a body of vested rights and intangible assets belonging to these special interests.

Of a similar character, in so far that in effect they are in the nature of sabotage—conscientious withdrawal of efficiency—are all manner of excise and revenue-stamp regulations; although they are not always designed for that purpose. Such would be, for instance, the partial or complete prohibition of alcoholic beverages, the regulation of the trade in tobacco, opium, and other deleterious narcotics, drugs, poisons, and high explosives. Of the same nature, in effect if not in intention, are such regulations as the oleomargarine law; as also the unnecessarily costly and vexatious routine of inspection imposed on the production of industrial (denatured) alcohol, which has inured to the benefit of certain business concerns that are interested in other fuels for use in internal-combustion engines; so also the singularly vexatious and elaborately imbecile specifications that limit and discourage the use of the parcel post, for the benefit of the express companies and other carriers which have a vested interest in traffic of that kind.

It is worth noting in the same connection, although it comes in from the other side of the case, that ever since the express companies have been taken over by the federal administration there has visibly gone into effect a comprehensive system of vexation and delay in the detail conduct of their traffic, so contrived as to discredit federal control of this traffic and thereby provoke a popular sentiment in favor of its early return to private control. Much the same state of things has been in evidence in the railway traffic under similar conditions. Sabotage is serviceable as a deterrent, whether in furtherance of the administration's work or in contravention of it.

In what has just been said there is, of course, no intention to find fault with any of these uses of sabotage. It is not a question of morals and good intentions. It is always to be presumed as a matter of course that the guiding spirit in all such governmental moves to regularize the nation's affairs, whether by restraint or by incitement, is a wise solicitude for the nation's enduring gain and security. All that can be said here is that many of these wise measures of restraint and incitement are in the nature of sabotage, and that in effect they habitually, though not invariably, inure to the benefit of certain vested interests—ordinarily vested interests which bulk large in the ownership and control of the nation's resources. That these measures are quite legitimate and presumably salutary, therefore, goes without saying. In effect they are measures for hindering traffic and industry at one point or another, which may often be a wise business precaution.

During the period of the war administrative measures in the nature of sabotage have been greatly extended in scope and kind. Peculiar and imperative exigencies have had to be met, and the staple means of meeting many of these new and exceptional exigencies has quite reasonably been something in the way of avoidance, disallowance, penalization, hindrance, a conscientious withdrawal of efficiency from work that does not fall in with the purposes of the Administration. Very much as is true in private business when a situation of doubt and hazard presents itself, so also in the business of government at the present juncture of exacting demands and inconvenient limitations, the Administration has been driven to expedients of disallowance and obstruction with regard to some of the ordinary processes of life, as, for instance, in the nonessential industries. It has also appeared that the ordinary equipment and agencies for gathering and distributing news and other information have in the past developed a capacity far in excess of what can safely be permitted in time of war or of returning peace. The like is true for the ordinary facilities for public discussion of all sorts of public questions. The ordinary facilities, which may have seemed scant enough in time of peace and slack interest, had after all developed a capacity far beyond what the governmental traffic will bear in these uneasy times of war and negotiations, when men are very much on the alert to know what is going on. By a moderate use of the later improvements in the technology of transport and communication, the ordinary means of disseminating information and opinions have grown so efficient that the traffic can no longer be allowed to run at full capacity during a period of stress in the business of government. Even the mail service has proved insufferably efficient, and a selective withdrawal of efficiency has gone into effect. To speak after the analogy of private business, it has been found best to disallow such use of the mail facilities as does not inure to the benefit of the Administration in the way of good will and vested rights of usufruct.

These peremptory measures of disallowance have attracted a wide and dubious attention; but they have doubtless been of a salutary nature and intention, in some way which is not to be understood by outsiders—that is to say, by citizens of the Republic. An unguarded dissemination of information and opinions or an unduly frank canvassing of the relevant facts by these outsiders, will be a handicap on the Administration's work, and may even defeat the Administration's aims. At least so they say.

Something of much the same color has been observed elsewhere and in other times, so that all this nervously alert resort to sabotage on undesirable information and opinions is nothing novel, nor is it peculiarly democratic. The elder statesmen of the great monarchies, east and west, have long seen and approved the like. But these elder statesmen of the dynastic régime have gone to their work of sabotage on information because of a palpable division of sentiment between their government and the underlying population, such as does not exist in the advanced democratic commonwealths. The case of Imperial Germany during the period of

the war is believed to show such a division of sentiment between the government and the underlying population, and
also to show how such a divided sentiment on the part of
a distrustful and distrusted population had best be dealt with.
The method approved by German dynastic experience is
sabotage, of a somewhat free-swung character, censorship,
embargo on communication, and also, it is confidently al-
leged, elaborate misinformation.

Such procedure on the part of the dynastic statesmen
of the Empire is comprehensible even to a layman. But how
it all stands with those advanced democratic nations, like
America, where the government is the dispassionately faithful
agent and spokesman of the body of citizens, and where
there can consequently be no division of aims and sentiment
between the body of officials and any underlying population
—all that is a more obscure and hazardous subject of speculation. Yet there has been censorship, somewhat rigorous,
and there has been selective refusal of mail facilities, somewhat arbitrary, in these democratic commonwealths also,
and not least in America, freely acknowledged to be the most
naïvely democratic of them all. And all the while one would
like to believe that it all has somehow served some useful
end. It is all sufficiently perplexing.

II

The Industrial System and the Captains of Industry

It has been usual, and indeed it still is not unusual, to speak of three coordinate "factors of production": land, labor, and capital. The reason for this threefold scheme of factors in production is that there have been three recognized classes of income: rent, wages, and profits; and it has been assumed that whatever yields an income is a productive factor. This scheme has come down from the eighteenth century. It is presumed to have been true, in a general way, under the conditions which prevailed in the eighteenth century, and it has therefore also been assumed that it should continue to be natural, or normal, true in some eminent sense, under any other conditions that have come on since that time.

Seen in the light of later events this threefold plan of coordinate factors in production is notable for what it omits. It assigns no productive effect to the industrial arts, for example, for the conclusive reason that the state of the industrial arts yields no stated or ratable income to any one class of persons; it affords no legal claim to a share in the community's yearly production of goods. The state of the industrial art is a joint stock of knowledge derived from past experience, and is held and passed on as an indivisible possession of the community at large. It is the indispensable foundation of all productive industry, of course, but except for certain minute fragments covered by patent rights or trade secrets, this joint stock is no man's individual property. For this reason it has not been counted in as a factor in production. The unexampled advance of technology during the past one hundred and fifty years has now begun to call attention to its omission from the threefold plan of productive factors handed down from that earlier time.

Another omission from the scheme of factors, as it was originally drawn, was the business man. But in the course of the nineteenth century the business man came more and more obtrusively to the front and came in for a more and more generous portion of the country's yearly income—which was taken to argue that he also contributed increasingly to the yearly production of goods. So a fourth factor of production has provisionally been added to the threefold scheme, in the person of the "entrepreneur," whose wages of management are considered to measure his creative share in the production of goods, although there still is some question as to the precise part of the entrepreneur in productive industry.

"Entrepreneur" is a technical term to designate the man who takes care of the financial end of things. It covers the same fact as the more familiar "business man," but with a vague suggestion of big business rather than small. The typical entrepreneur is the corporation financier. And since the corporation financier has habitually come in for a very substantial share of the community's yearly income he has also been conceived to render a very substantial service to the community as a creative force in that productive industry out of which the yearly income arises. Indeed, it is nearly true that in current usage "producer" has come to mean "financial manager," both in the standard economic theory and in everyday speech.

There need of course be no quarrel with all this. It is a matter of usage. During the era of the machine industry— which is also the era of the commercial democracy—business men have controlled production and have managed the industry of the commonwealth for their own ends, so that the material fortunes of all the civilized peoples have continued to turn on the financial management of their business men. And during the same period not only have the conditions of life among these civilized peoples continued to be fairly tolerable on the whole, but it is also true that the industrial system which these business men have been managing for their own private gain all this time has continually been growing more efficient on the whole. Its productive capacity per unit of equipment and man power has continually grown larger. For this very creditable outcome due credit should be, as indeed it has been, given to the business community which has had the oversight of things. The efficient enlargement of industrial capacity has, of course, been due to a continued advance in technology, to a continued increase of the available natural resources, and to a continued increase of population. But the business community have also had a part in bringing all this to pass; they have always been in a position to hinder this growth, and it is only by their consent and advice that things have been enabled to go forward so far as they have gone.

This sustained advance in productive capacity, due to the continued advance in technology and in population, has also had another notable consequence. According to the Liberal principles of the eighteenth century any legally defensible receipt of income is a sure sign of productive work done. Seen in the light of this assumption, the visibly increasing productive capacity of the industrial system has enabled all men of a liberal and commercial mind not only to credit the businesslike captains of industry with having created this productive capacity, but also to overlook all that the same captains of industry have been doing in the ordinary course of business to hold productive industry in check. And it happens that all this time things have been moving in such a direction and have now gone so far that it is today quite an open question whether the businesslike management of the captains is not more occupied with checking industry than with increasing its productive capacity.

This captain of industry, typified by the corporation financier, and latterly by the investment banker, is one of the institutions that go to make up the new order of things, which has been coming on among all the civilized peoples ever since the Industrial Revolution set in. As such, as an institutional growth, his life history hitherto should be worth looking into for any one who proposes to understand the recent growth and present drift of this new economic order. The beginnings of the captain of industry are to be seen at their best among those enterprising Englishmen who made it their work to carry the industrial promise of the Revolution out into tangible performance, during the closing decades of the eighteenth and the early decades of the nineteenth century. These captains of the early time are likely to be rated as inventors, at least in a loose sense of the word. But it is more to the point that they were designers and builders of factory, mill, and mine equipment, of engines, processes, machines, and machine tools, as well as shop managers, at the same time that they took care, more or less effectually, of the financial end. Nowhere do these beginnings of the captain of industry stand out so convincingly as among the English tool-builders of that early time, who designed, tried out, built, and marketed that series of indispensable machine tools that has made the practical foundation of the mechanical industry. Something to much the same effect is due to be said for the pioneering work of the Americans along the same general lines of mechanical design and performance at a slightly later period. To men of this class the new industrial order owes much of its early success as well as of its later growth.

These men were captains of industry, entrepreneurs, in some such simple and comprehensive sense of the word as that which the economists appear to have had in mind for a hundred years after, when they have spoken of the wages of management that are due the entrepreneur for productive work done. They were a cross between a business man and an industrial expert, and the industrial expert appears to have been the more valuable half in their composition. But factory, mine, and ship owners, as well as merchants and bankers, also made up a vital part of that business community out of whose later growth and specialization the corporation finan- cier of the nineteenth and twentieth centuries has arisen. His origins are both technological and commercial, and in that early phase of his life history which has been taken over into the traditions of economic theory and of common sense he carried on both of these lines of interest and of work in com- bination. That was before the large scale, the wide sweep, and the profound specialization of the advanced mechanical industry had gathered headway.

But progressively the cares of business management grew larger and more exacting, as the scale of things in business grew larger, and so the directive head of any such business concern came progressively to give his attention more and more exclusively to the "financial end." At the same time and driven by the same considerations the businesslike man- agement of industry has progressively been shifting to the footing of corporation finance. This has brought on a further division, dividing the ownership of the industrial equipment and resources from their management. But also at the same time the industrial system, on its technological side, has been progressively growing greater and going farther in scope, diversity, specialization, and complexity, as well as in pro- ductive capacity per unit of equipment and man power.

The last named item of change, the progressive increase of productive capacity, is peculiarly significant in this con- nection. Through the earlier and pioneering decades of the machine era it appears to have been passably true that the ordinary routine of management in industrial business was taken up with reaching out for new ways and means and speeding up production to maximum capacity. That was be- fore standardization of processes and of unit products and fabrication of parts had been carried far, and therefore be- fore quantity production had taken on anything like its later range and reach. And, partly because of that fact—because quantity production was then still a slight matter and greatly circumscribed, as contrasted with its later growth—the ordinary volume of output in the mechanical industries was still relatively slight and manageable. Therefore those concerns that were engaged in these industries still had a fairly open market for whatever they might turn out, a market capable of taking up any reasonable increase of output. Exceptions to this general rule occurred; as, e.g., in textiles. But the general rule stands out obtrusively through the early decades of the nineteenth century so far as regards English industry, and even more obviously in the case of America. Such an open market meant a fair chance for competitive production, without too much risk of overstocking. And running to the same effect, there was the continued increase of population and the continually increasing reach and volume of the means of transport, serving to maintain a free market for any prospective increase of output, at prices which offered a fair prospect of continued profit. In the degree in which this condition of things prevailed a reasonably free competitive production would be practicable.

The industrial situation so outlined began visibly to give way toward the middle of the nineteenth century in England, and at a correspondingly later period in America. The productive capacity of the mechanical industry was visibly overtaking the capacity of the market, so that free competition without afterthought was no longer a sound footing on which to manage production. Loosely, this critical or transitional period falls in and about the second quarter of the nineteenth century in England; elsewhere at a correspondingly later date. Of course the critical point, when business exigencies began to dictate a policy of combination and restriction, did not come at the same date in all or in most of the mechanical industries; but it seems possible to say that, by and large, the period of transition to a general rule of restriction in industry comes on at the time and for the reason so indicated. There were also other factors engaged in that industrial situation, besides those spoken of above, less notable and less sharply defined, but enforcing limitations of the same character. Such were, e.g., a rapidly gaining obsolescence of industrial plant, due to improvements and extensions, as also the partial exhaustion of the labor supply by persistent overwork, under-feeding, and unsanitary conditions—but this applies to the English case rather than elsewhere.

In point of time this critical period in the affairs of industrial business coincides roughly with the coming in of corporation finance as the ordinary and typical method of controlling the industrial output. Of course the corporation, or company, has other uses besides the restrictive control of the output with a view to a profitable market, but it should be sufficiently obvious that the combination of ownership and centralization of control which the corporation brings about is also exceedingly convenient for that purpose. And when it appears that the general resort to corporate organization of the larger sort sets in about the time when business exigencies begin to dictate an imperative restriction of output, it is not easy to avoid the conclusion that this was one of the ends to be served by this reorganization of business enterprise. Business enterprise may fairly be said to have shifted from the footing of free-swung competitive production to that of a "conscientious withholding of efficiency," so soon and so far as corporation finance on a sufficiently large scale had come to be the controlling factor in industry. At the same time and in the same degree the discretionary control of industry, and of other business enterprise in great part, has passed into the hands of the corporation financier.

Corporate organization has continually gone forward to a larger scale and a more comprehensive coalition of forces, and at the same time, and more and more visibly, it has become the ordinary duty of the corporate management to adjust production to the requirements of the market by restricting the output to what the traffic will bear; that is to say, what will yield the largest net earnings. Under corporate management it rarely happens that production is pushed to the limit of capacity. It happens, and can happen, only rarely and intermittently. This has been true, increasingly, ever since the ordinary productive capacity of the mechanical industries seriously began to overtake and promised to exceed what the market would carry off at a reasonably profitable price. And ever since that critical turn in the affairs of industrial business—somewhere in the middle half of the nineteenth century—it has become increasingly imperative to use a wise moderation and stop down the output to such a rate and volume as the traffic will bear. The cares of business have required an increasingly undivided attention on the part of the business men, and in an ever increasing measure their day's work has come to center about a running adjustment of sabotage on production. And for this purpose, evidently, the corporate organization of this business, on an increasingly large scale, is very serviceable, since the requisite sabotage on productive industry can be effectually administered only on a large plan and with a firm hand.

"The leaders in business are men who have studied and thought all their lives. They have thus learned to decide big problems at once, basing their decisions upon their knowledge of fundamental principles."—Jeremiah W. Jenks, That is to say, the surveillance of this financial end of industrial business, and the control of the requisite running balance of sabotage, have been reduced to a routine governed by settled principles of procedure and administered by suitably trained experts in corporation finance. But under the limitations to which all human capacity is subject it follows from this increasingly exacting discipline of business administration that the business men are increasingly out of touch with that manner of thinking and those elements of knowledge that go to make up the logic and the relevant facts of the mechanical technology. Addiction to a strict and unremitting valuation of all things in terms of price and profit leaves them, by settled habit, unfit to appreciate those technological facts and values that can be formulated only in terms of tangible mechanical performance; increasingly so with every further move into a stricter addiction to business-like management and with every further advance of the industrial system into a still wider scope and a still more diversified and more delicately balanced give and take among its interlocking members.

They are experts in prices and profits and financial manœuvres; and yet the final discretion in all questions of industrial policy continues to rest in their hands. They are by training and interest captains of finance; and yet, with no competent grasp of the industrial arts, they continue to exercise a plenary discretion as captains of industry. They are unremittingly engaged in a routine of acquisition, in which they habitually reach their ends by a shrewd restriction of output; and yet they continue to be entrusted with the community's industrial welfare, which calls for maximum production.

Such has been the situation in all the civilized countries since corporation finance has ruled industry, and until a recent date. Quite recently this settled scheme of business management has shown signs of giving way, and a new move in the organization of business enterprise has come in sight, whereby the discretionary control of industrial production is shifting still farther over to the side of finance and still farther out of touch with the requirements of maximum production. The new move is of a twofold character: (a) the financial captains of industry have been proving their industrial incompetence in a progressively convincing fashion, and (b) their own proper work of financial management has progressively taken on a character of standardized routine such as no longer calls for or admits any large measure of discretion or initiative. They have been losing touch with the management of industrial processes, at the same time that the management of corporate business has, in effect, been shifting into the hands of a bureaucratic clerical staff. The corporation financier of popular tradition is taking on the character of a chief of bureau.

The changes which have brought the corporation financier to this somewhat inglorious position of a routine administrator set in along with the early growth of corporation finance, somewhere around the middle of the nineteenth century, and they have come to a head somewhere about the passage to the twentieth century, although it is only since the latter date that the outcome is becoming at all clearly defined. When corporate organization and the consequent control of output came into bearing there were two lines of policy open to the management: (a) to maintain profitable prices by limiting the output, and (b) to maintain profits by lowering the production costs of an increased output. To some extent both of these lines were followed, but on the whole the former proved the more attractive; it involved less risk, and it required less acquaintance with the working processes of industry. At least it appears that in effect the preference was increasingly given to the former method during this half-century of financial management. For this there were good reasons. The processes of production were continually growing more extensive, diversified, complicated, and more difficult for any layman in technology to comprehend—and the corporation financier was such a layman, necessarily and increasingly so, for reasons indicated above. At the same time, owing to a continued increase of population and a continued extension of the industrial system, the net product of industry and its net earnings continued to increase independently of any creative effort on the part of the financial management. So the corporation financier, as a class, came in for an "unearned increment" of income, on the simple plan of "sitting tight." That plan is intelligible to any layman. All industrial innovation and all aggressive economy in the conduct of industry not only presumes an insight into the technological details of the industrial process, but to any other than the technological experts, who know the facts intimately, any move of that kind will appear hazardous. So the business men who have controlled industry, being laymen in all that concerns its management, have increasingly been content to let well enough alone and to get along with an ever increasing overhead charge of inefficiency, so long as they have lost nothing by it. The result has been an ever increasing volume of waste and misdirection in the use of equipment, resources, and man power throughout the industrial system.

In time, that is to say within the last few years, the resulting lag, leak, and friction in the ordinary working of this mechanical industry under business management have reached such proportions that no ordinarily intelligent outsider can help seeing them wherever he may look into the facts of the case. But it is the industrial experts, not the business men, who have finally begun to criticize this businesslike mismanagement and neglect of the ways and means of industry. And hitherto their efforts and advice have met with no cordial response from the business men in charge, who have, on the whole, continued to let well enough alone— that is to say, what is well enough for a short-sighted business policy looking to private gain, however poorly it may serve the material needs of the community. But in the meantime two things have been happening which have deranged the régime of the corporation financier: industrial experts, engineers, chemists, mineralogists, technicians of all kinds, have been drifting into more responsible positions in the industrial system and have been growing up and multiplying within the system, because the system will no longer work at all without them; and on the other hand, the large financial interests on whose support the corporation financiers have been leaning have gradually come to realize that corporation finance can best be managed as a comprehensive bureaucratic routine, and that the two pillars of the house of corporate business enterprise of the larger sort are the industrial experts and the large financial concerns that control the necessary funds; whereas the corporation financier is little more than a dubious intermediate term between these two.

One of the greater personages in American business finance took note of this situation in the late nineties and set about turning it to account for the benefit of himself and his business associates, and from that period dates a new era in American corporation finance. It was for a time spoken of loosely as the Era of Trust-Making, but that phrase does not describe it at all adequately. It should rather be called the Era of the Investment Banker, and it has come to its present stage of maturity and stability only in the course of the past quarter-century.

The characteristic features and the guiding purpose of this improved method in corporation finance are best shown by a showing of the methods and achievements of that great pioneer by whom it was inaugurated. As an illustrative case, then, the American steel business in the nineties was suffering from the continued use of out-of-date processes, equipment, and locations, from wasteful management under the control of stubbornly ignorant corporation officials, and particularly from intermittent haphazard competition and mutual sabotage between the numerous concerns which were then doing business in steel. It appears to have been the last-named difficulty that particularly claimed the attention and supplied the opportunity of the great pioneer. He can by no stretch of charity be assumed to have had even a slight acquaintance with the technological needs and shortcomings of the steel industry. But to a man of commercial vision and financial sobriety it was plain that a more comprehensive, and therefore more authoritative, organization and control of the steel business would readily obviate much of the competition which was deranging prices. The apparent purpose and the evident effect of the new and larger coalition of business interests in steel was to maintain profitable prices by a reasonable curtailment of production. A secondary and less evident effect was a more economical management of the industry, which involved some displacement of quondam corporation financiers and some introduction of industrial experts. A further, but unavowed, end to be served by the same move in each of the many enterprises in coalition undertaken by the great pioneer and by his competitors was a bonus that came to these enterprising men in the shape of an increased capitalization of the business. But the notable feature of it all as seen from the point of view of the public at large was always the stabilization of prices at a reasonably high level, such as would always assure reasonably large earnings on the increased capitalization.

Since then this manner of corporation finance has been further perfected and standardized, until it will now hold true that no large move in the field of corporation finance can be made without the advice and consent of those large funded interests that are in a position to act as investment bankers; nor does any large enterprise in corporation business ever escape from the continued control of the investment bankers in any of its larger transactions; nor can any corporate enterprise of the larger sort now continue to do business except on terms which will yield something appreciable in the way of income to the investment bankers, whose continued support is necessary to its success.

The financial interest here spoken of as the investment banker is commonly something in the way of a more or less articulate syndicate of financial houses, and it is to be added that the same financial concerns are also commonly, if not invariably, engaged or interested in commercial banking of the usual kind. So that the same well-established, half-syndicated ramification of banking houses that have been taking care of the country's commercial banking, with its center of credit and of control at the country's financial metropolis, is ready from beforehand to take over and administer the country's corporation finance on a unified plan and with a view to an equitable distribution of the country's net earnings among themselves and their clients. The more inclusive this financial organization is, of course, the more able it will be to manage the country's industrial system as an inclusive whole and prevent any hazardous innovation or experiment, as well as to limit production of the necessaries to such a volume of output as will yield the largest net return to itself and its clients.

Evidently the improved plan which has thrown the discretion and responsibility into the hands of the investment banker should make for a safe and sound conduct of business, such as will avoid fluctuations of price, and more particularly avoid any unprofitable speeding-up of productive industry. Evidently, too, the initiative has hereby passed out of the hands of the corporation financier, who has fallen into the position of a financial middleman or agent, with limited discretion and with a precariously doubtful future. But all human institutions are susceptible of improvement, and the course of improvement may now and again, as in his case, result in supersession and displacement. And doubtless it is all for the best, that is to say, for the good of business, more particularly for the profit of big business.

But now as always corporation finance is a traffic credit; indeed, now more than ever before. Therefore to stabilize corporate business sufficiently in the hands of this inclusive quasi-syndicate of banking interests it is necessary that the credit system of the country should as a whole be administered on a unified plan and inclusively. All of which is taken care of by the same conjunction of circumstances; the same quasi-syndicate of banking interests that makes use of the country's credit in the way of corporation finance is also the guardian of the country's credit at large. From which it results that, as regards those large-scale credit extensions which are of substantial consequence, the credits and debits are, in effect, pooled within the syndicate, so that no substantial derangement of the credit situation can take effect except by the free choice of this quasi-syndicate of investment banking houses; that is to say, not except they see an advantage to themselves in allowing the credit situation to be deranged, and not beyond the point which will best serve their collective purpose as against the rest of the community. With such a closed system no extension of credit obligations or multiplication of corporate securities, with the resulting inflation of values, need bring any risk of a liquidation, since credits and debits are in effect pooled within the system. By way of parenthesis it may also be remarked that under these circumstances "credit" has no particular meaning except as a method of accounting. Credit is also one of the timeworn institutions that are due to suffer obsolescence by improvement.

This process of pooling and syndication that is remaking the world of credit and corporation finance has been greatly helped on in America by the establishment of the Federal Reserve system, while somewhat similar results have been achieved elsewhere by somewhat similar devices. That system has greatly helped to extend, facilitate, simplify, and consolidate the unified control of the country's credit arrangements, and it has very conveniently left the substantial control in the hands of those larger financial interests into whose hands the lines of control in credit and industrial business were already being gathered by force of circumstances and by sagacious management of the interested parties. By this means the substantial core of the country's credit system is gathered into a self-balanced whole, closed and unbreakable, self-insured against all risk and derangement. All of which converges to the definitive stabilization of the country's business; but since it reduces financial traffic to a riskless routine it also converges to the conceivable obsolescence of corporation finance and eventually, perhaps, of the investment banker.

III

The Captains
of Finance
and the Engineers

I*n more than one respect the industrial system of today* is notably different from anything that has gone before. It is eminently a system, self-balanced and comprehensive; and it is a system of interlocking mechanical processes, rather than of skilful manipulation. It is mechanical rather than manual. It is an organization of mechanical powers and material resources, rather than of skilled craftsmen and tools; although the skilled workmen and tools are also an indispensable part of its comprehensive mechanism. It is of an impersonal nature, after the fashion of the material sciences, on which it constantly draws. It runs to "quantity production" of specialized and standardized goods and services. For all these reasons it lends itself to systematic control under the direction of industrial experts, skilled technologists, who may be called "production engineers," for want of a better term.

This industrial system runs on as an inclusive organization of many and diverse interlocking mechanical processes, interdependent and balanced among themselves in such a way that the due working of any part of it is conditioned on the due working of all the rest. Therefore it will work at its best only on condition that these industrial experts, production engineers, will work together on a common understanding; and more particularly on condition that they must not work at cross purposes. These technological specialists whose constant supervision is indispensable to the due working of the industrial system constitute the general staff of industry, whose work it is to control the strategy of production at large and to keep an oversight of the tactics of production in detail.

Such is the nature of this industrial system on whose due working depends the material welfare of all the civilized peoples. It is an inclusive system drawn on a plan of strict and comprehensive interdependence, such that, in point of material welfare, no nation and no community has anything to gain at the cost of any other nation or community. In point of material welfare, all the civilized peoples have been drawn together by the state of the industrial arts into a single going concern. And for the due working of this inclusive going concern it is essential that that corps of technological specialists who by training, insight, and interest make up the general staff of industry must have a free hand in the disposal of its available resources, in materials, equipment, and man power, regardless of any national pretensions or any vested interests. Any degree of obstruction, diversion, or withholding of any of the available industrial forces, with a view to the special gain of any nation or any investor, unavoidably brings on a dislocation of the system; which involves a disproportionate lowering of its working efficiency and therefore a disproportionate loss to the whole, and therefore a net loss to all its parts.

And all the while the statesmen are at work to divert and obstruct the working forces of this industrial system, here and there, for the special advantage of one nation and another at the cost of the rest; and the captains of finance are working, at cross purposes and in collusion, to divert whatever they can to the special gain of one vested interest and another, at any cost to the rest. So it happens that the industrial system is deliberately handicapped with dissension, misdirection, and unemployment of material resources, equipment, and man power, at every turn where the statesmen or the captains of finance can touch its mechanism; and all the civilized peoples are suffering privation together because their general staff of industrial experts are in this way required to take orders and submit to sabotage at the hands of the statesmen and the vested interests. Politics and investment are still allowed to decide matters of industrial policy which should plainly be left to the discretion of the general staff of production engineers driven by no commercial bias.

No doubt this characterization of the industrial system and its besetting tribulations will seem overdrawn. However, it is not intended to apply to any date earlier than the twentieth century, or to any backward community that still lies outside the sweep of the mechanical industry. Only gradually during the past century, while the mechanical industry has progressively been taking over the production of goods and services, and going over to quantity production, has the industrial system taken on this character of an inclusive organization of interlocking processes and interchange of materials; and it is only in the twentieth century that this cumulative progression has come to a head with such effect that this characterization is now visibly becoming true. And even now it will hold true, visibly and securely, only as applies to the leading mechanical industries, those main lines of industry that shape the main conditions of life, and in which quantity production has become the common and indispensable rule. Such are, e.g., transport and communication; the production and industrial use of coal, oil, electricity and water power; the production of steel and other metals; of wood pulp, lumber, cement and other building materials; of textiles and rubber; as also grain-milling and much of the grain-growing, together with meat-packing and a good share of the stock-raising industry.

There is, of course, a large volume of industry in many lines which has not, or only in part and doubtfully, been drawn into this network of mechanical processes and quantity production, in any direct and conclusive fashion. But these other lines of industry that still stand over on another

and older plan of operation are, after all, outliers and subsidiaries of the mechanically organized industrial system, dependent on or subservient to those greater underlying industries which make up the working body of the system, and
which therefore set the pace for the rest. And in the main,
therefore, and as regards these greater mechanical industries
on whose due working the material welfare of the community
depends from day to day, this characterization will apply
without material abatement.

But it should be added that even as regards these
greater, primary and underlying, lines of production the system has not yet reached a fatal degree of close-knit interdependence, balance, and complication; it will still run along
at a very tolerable efficiency in the face of a very appreciable
amount of persistent derangement. That is to say, the industrial system at large has not yet become so delicately balanced a mechanical structure and process that the ordinary
amount of derangement and sabotage necessary to the ordinary control of production by business methods will para-
lyze the whole outright. The industrial system is not yet sufficiently close-knit for that. And yet, that extent and degree
of paralysis from which the civilized world's industry is
suffering just now, due to legitimate businesslike sabotage,
goes to argue that the date may not be far distant when the
interlocking processes of the industrial system shall have
become so closely interdependent and so delicately balanced
that even the ordinary modicum of sabotage involved in the
conduct of business as usual will bring the whole to a fatal
collapse. The derangement and privation brought on by any
well organized strike of the larger sort argues to the same
effect.

In effect, the progressive advance of this industrial system towards an all-inclusive mechanical balance of interlocking processes appears to be approaching a critical pass,
beyond which it will no longer be practicable to leave its control in the hands of business men working at cross purposes

for private gain, or to entrust its continued administration to others than suitably trained technological experts, production engineers without a commercial interest. What these men may then do with it all is not so plain; the best they can do may not be good enough; but the negative proposition is becoming sufficiently plain, that this mechanical state of the industrial arts will not long tolerate the continued control of production by the vested interests under the current business-like rule of incapacity by advisement.

In the beginning, that is to say during the early growth of the machine industry, and particularly in that new growth of mechanical industries which arose directly out of the Industrial Revolution, there was no marked division between the industrial experts and the business managers. That was before the new industrial system had gone far on the road of progressive specialization and complexity, and before business had reached an exactingly large scale; so that even the business men of that time, who were without special training in technological matters, would still be able to exercise something of an intelligent oversight of the whole, and to understand something of what was required in the mechanical conduct of the work which they financed and from which they drew their income. Not unusually the designers of industrial processes and equipment would then still take care of the financial end, at the same time that they managed the shop. But from an early point in the development there set in a progressive differentiation, such as to divide those who designed and administered the industrial processes from those others who designed and managed the commercial transactions and took care of the financial end. So there also set in a corresponding division of powers between the business management and the technological experts. It became the work of the technologist to determine, on technological grounds, what could be done in the way of productive industry, and to contrive ways and means of doing it; but the business management always continued to decide, on commercial grounds, how much work should be done and what kind and quality of goods and services should be produced; and the decision of the business management has always continued to be final, and has always set the limit beyond which production must not go.

With the continued growth of specialization the experts have necessarily had more and more to say in the affairs of industry; but always their findings as to what work is to be done and what ways and means are to be employed in production have had to wait on the findings of the business managers as to what will be expedient for the purpose of commercial gain. This division between business management and industrial management has continued to go forward, at a continually accelerated rate, because the special training and experience required for any passably efficient organization and direction of these industrial processes has continually grown more exacting, calling for special knowledge and abilities on the part of those who have this work to do and requiring their undivided interest and their undivided attention to the work in hand. But these specialists in technological knowledge, abilities, interest, and experience, who have increasingly come into the case in this way—inventors, designers, chemists, mineralogists, soil experts, crop specialists, production managers and engineers of many kinds and denominations—have continued to be employees of the captains of industry, that is to say, of the captains of finance, whose work it has been to commercialize the knowledge and abilities of the industrial experts and turn them to account for their own gain.

It is perhaps unnecessary to add the axiomatic corollary that the captains have always turned the technologists and their knowledge to account in this way only so far as would serve their own commercial profit, not to the extent of their ability; or to the limit set by the material circumstances; or by the needs of the community. The result has been, uniformly and as a matter of course, that the production of goods and services has advisedly been stopped short of productive capacity, by curtailment of output and by derangement of the productive system. There are two main reasons for this, and both have operated together throughout the machine era to stop industrial production increasingly short of productive capacity. (a) The commercial need of maintaining a profitable price has led to an increasingly imperative curtailment of the output, as fast as the advance of the industrial arts has enhanced the productive capacity. And (b) the continued advance of the mechanical technology has called for an ever-increasing volume and diversity of special knowledge, and so has left the businesslike captains of finance continually farther in arrears, so that they have been less and less capable of comprehending what is required in the ordinary way of industrial equipment and personnel. They have therefore, in effect, maintained prices at a profitable level by curtailment of output rather than by lowering production-cost per unit of output, because they have not had such a working acquaintance with the technological facts in the case as would enable them to form a passably sound judgment of suitable ways and means for lowering production-cost; and at the same time, being shrewd business men, they have been unable to rely on the hired-man's-loyalty of technologists whom they do not understand. The result has been a somewhat distrustful blindfold choice of processes and personnel and a consequent enforced incompetence in the management of industry, a curtailment of output below the needs of the community, below the productive capacity of the industrial system, and below what an intelligent control of production would have made commercially profitable.

Through the earlier decades of the machine era these limitations imposed on the work of the experts by the demands of profitable business and by the technical ignorance of the business men, appears not to have been a heavy handicap, whether as a hindrance to the continued development of technological knowledge or as an obstacle to its ordinary use in industry. That was before the mechanical industry had gone far in scope, complexity, and specialization; and it was also before the continued work of the technologists had pushed the industrial system to so high a productive capacity that it is forever in danger of turning out a larger product than is required for a profitable business. But gradually, with the passage of time and the advance of the industrial arts to a wider scope and a larger scale, and to an increasing specialization and standardization of processes, the technological knowledge that makes up the state of the industrial arts has called for a higher degree of that training that makes industrial specialists; and at the same time any passably efficient management of industry has of necessity drawn on them and their special abilities to an ever-increasing extent. At the same time and by the same shift of circumstances, the captains of finance, driven by an increasingly close application to the affairs of business, have been going farther out of touch with the ordinary realities of productive industry; and it is to be admitted, they have also continued increasingly to distrust the technological specialists, whom they do not understand, but whom they can also not get along without. The captains have per force continued to employ the technologists, to make money for them, but they have done so only reluctantly, tardily, sparingly, and with a shrewd circumspection; only because and so far as they have been persuaded that the use of these technologists was indispensable to the making of money.

One outcome of this persistent and pervasive tardiness and circumspection on the part of the captains has been an incredibly and increasingly uneconomical use of material resources, and an incredibly wasteful organization of equipment and man power in those great industries where the technological advance has been most marked. In good part it was this discreditable pass, to which the leading industries had been brought by these one-eyed captains of industry, that brought the régime of the captains to an inglorious close, by shifting the initiative and discretion in this domain out of their hands into those of the investment bankers. By custom the investment bankers had occupied a position between or overlapping the duties of a broker in corporate securities and those of an underwriter of corporate flotations—such a position, in effect, as is still assigned them in the standard writings on corporation finance. The increasingly large scale of corporate enterprise, as well as the growth of a mutual understanding among these business concerns, also had its share in this new move. But about this time, too, the "consulting engineers" were coming notably into evidence in many of those lines of industry in which corporation finance has habitually been concerned.

So far as concerns the present argument the ordinary duties of these consulting engineers have been to advise the investment bankers as to the industrial and commercial soundness, past and prospective, of any enterprise that is to be underwritten. These duties have comprised a painstaking and impartial examination of the physical properties involved in any given case, as well as an equally impartial auditing of the accounts and appraisal of the commercial promise of such enterprises, for the guidance of the bankers or syndicate of bankers interested in the case as underwriters. On this ground working arrangements and a mutual understanding presently arose between the consulting engineers and those banking houses that habitually were concerned in the underwriting of corporate enterprises.

The effect of this move has been twofold: experience has brought out the fact that corporation finance, at its best and soundest, has now become a matter of comprehensive and standardized bureaucratic routine, necessarily comprising the mutual relations between various corporate concerns, and best to be taken care of by a clerical staff of trained accountants; and the same experience has put the financial houses in direct touch with the technological general staff of the industrial system, whose surveillance has become increasingly imperative to the conduct of any profitable enterprise in industry. But also, by the same token, it has appeared that the corporation financier of nineteenth-century tradition is no longer of the essence of the case in corporation finance of the larger and more responsible sort. He has, in effect, come to be no better than an idle wheel in the economic mechanism, serving only to take up some of the lubricant.

Since and so far as this shift out of the nineteenth century into the twentieth has been completed, the corporation financier has ceased to be a captain of industry and has become a lieutenant of finance; the captaincy having been taken over by the syndicated investment bankers and administered as a standardized routine of accountancy, having to do with the flotation of corporation securities and with their fluctuating values, and having also something to do with regulating the rate and volume of output in those industrial enterprises which so have passed under the hand of the investment bankers.

By and large, such is the situation of the industrial system today, and of that financial business that controls the industrial system. But this state of things is not so much an accomplished fact handed on out of the recent past; it is only that such is the culmination in which it all heads up in the immediate present, and that such is the visible drift of things into the calculable future. Only during the last few years has the state of affairs in industry been obviously falling into the shape so outlined, and it is even yet only in those larger and pace-making lines of industry which are altogether of the new technological order that the state of things has reached this finished shape. But in these larger and underlying divisions of the industrial system the present posture and drift of things is unmistakable. Meantime very much still stands over out of that régime of rule-of-thumb, competitive sabotage, and commercial log-rolling, in which the businesslike captains of the old order are so altogether well at home, and which has been the best that the captains have known how to contrive for the management of that industrial system whose captains they have been. So that wherever the production experts are now taking over the management, out of the dead hand of the self-made captains, and wherever they have occasions to inquire into the established conditions of production, they find the ground cumbered with all sorts of incredible makeshifts of waste and inefficiency—such makeshifts as would perhaps pass muster with any moderately stupid elderly layman, but which look like blindfold guesswork to these men who know something of the advanced technology and its working-out.

Hitherto, then, the growth and conduct of this industrial system presents this singular outcome. The technology—the state of the industrial arts—which takes effect in this mechanical industry is in an eminent sense a joint stock of knowledge and experience held in common by the civilized peoples. It requires the use of trained and instructed workmen—born, bred, trained, and instructed at the cost of the people at large. So also it requires, with a continually more exacting insistence, a corps of highly trained and specially gifted experts, of divers and various kinds. These, too, are born, bred, and trained at the cost of the community at large, and they draw their requisite special knowledge from the community's joint stock of accumulated experience. These expert men, technologists, engineers, or whatever name may best suit them, make up the indispensable General Staff of the industrial system; and without their immediate and unremitting guidance and correction the industrial system will not work. It is a mechanically organized structure of technical processes designed, installed, and conducted by these production engineers. Without them and their constant attention the industrial equipment, the mechanical appliances of industry, will foot up to just so much junk. The material welfare of the community is unreservedly bound up with the due working of this industrial system, and therefore with its unreserved control by the engineers, who alone are competent to manage it. To do their work as it should be done these men of the industrial general staff must have a free hand, unhampered by commercial considerations and reservations; for the production of the goods and services needed by the community they neither need nor are they in any degree benefited by any supervision or interference from the side of the owners. Yet the absentee owners, now represented, in effect, by the syndicated investment bankers, continue to control the industrial experts and limit their discretion, arbitrarily, for their own commercial gain, regardless of the needs of the community.

Hitherto these men who so make up the general staff of the industrial system have not drawn together into anything like a self-directing working force; nor have they been vested with anything more than an occasional, haphazard, and tentative control of some disjointed sector of the industrial equipment, with no direct or decisive relation to that personnel of productive industry that may be called the officers of the line and the rank and file. It is still the unbroken privilege of the financial management and its financial agents to "hire and fire." The final disposition of all the industrial forces still remains in the hands of the business men, who still continue to dispose of these forces for other than industrial ends. And all the while it is an open secret that with a reasonably free hand the production experts would today readily increase the ordinary output of industry by several fold,—variously estimated at some 300 per cent. to 1200 per cent. of the current output. And what stands in the way of so increasing the ordinary output of goods and services is business as usual.

Right lately these technologists have begun to become

uneasily "class-conscious" and to reflect that they together constitute the indispensable General Staff of the industrial system. Their class consciousness has taken the immediate form of a growing sense of waste and confusion in the management of industry by the financial agents of the absentee owners. They are beginning to take stock of that all-pervading mismanagement of industry that is inseparable from its control for commercial ends. All of which brings home a realization of their own shame and of damage to the common good. So the engineers are beginning to draw together and ask themselves, "What about it?"

This uneasy movement among the technologists set in, in an undefined and fortuitous way, in the closing years of the nineteenth century; when the consulting engineers, and then presently the "efficiency engineers," began to make scattered corrections in detail, which showed up the industrial incompetence of those elderly laymen who were doing a conservative business at the cost of industry. The consulting engineers of the standard type, both then and since then, are commercialized technologists, whose work it is to appraise the industrial value of any given enterprise with a view to its commercial exploitation. They are a cross between a technological specialist and a commercial agent, beset with the limitations of both and commonly not fully competent in either line. Their normal position is that of an employee of the investment bankers, on a stipend or a retainer, and it has ordinarily been their fortune to shift over in time from a technological footing to a frankly commercial one. The case of the efficiency engineers, or scientific-management experts, is somewhat similar. They too have set out to appraise, exhibit, and correct the commercial short-comings of the ordinary management of those industrial establishments which they investigate, to persuade the business men in charge how they may reasonably come in for larger net earnings by a more closely shorn exploitation of the industrial forces at their disposal. During the opening years of the new century a lively interest centered on the views and expositions of these two groups of industrial experts; and not least was the interest aroused by their exhibits of current facts indicating an all-pervading lag, leak, and friction in the industrial system, due to its disjointed and one-eyed management by commercial adventurers bent on private gain.

During these few years of the opening century the members of this informal guild of engineers at large have been taking an interest in this question of habitual mismanagement by ignorance and commercial sabotage, even apart from the commercial imbecility of it all. But it is the young rather than the old among them who see industry in any other light than its commercial value. Circumstances have decided that the older generation of the craft have become pretty well commercialized. Their habitual outlook has been shaped by a long and unbroken apprenticeship to the corporation financiers and the investment bankers; so that they still habitually see the industrial system as a contrivance for the roundabout process of making money. Accordingly, the established official Associations and Institutes of Engineers, which are officered and engineered by the elder engineers, old and young, also continue to show the commercial bias of their creators, in what they criticize and in what they propose. But the new generation which has been coming on during the present century are not similarly true to that tradition of commercial engineering that makes the technological man an awestruck lieutenant of the captain of finance.

By training, and perhaps also by native bent, the technologists find it easy and convincing to size up men and things in terms of tangible performance, without commercial afterthought, except so far as their apprenticeship to the captains of finance may have made commercial afterthought a second nature to them. Many of the younger generation are beginning to understand that engineering begins and ends in the domain of tangible performance, and that commercial expediency is another matter. Indeed, they are beginning to understand that commercial expediency has nothing better to contribute to the engineer's work than so much lag, leak, and friction. The four years' experience of the war has also been highly instructive on that head. So they are beginning to draw together on a common ground of understanding, as men who are concerned with the ways and means of tangible performance in the way of productive industry, according to the state of the industrial arts as they know them at their best; and there is a growing conviction among them that they together constitute the sufficient and indispensable general staff of the mechanical industries, on whose unhindered team-work depends the due working of the industrial system and therefore also the material welfare of the civilized peoples. So also, to these men who are trained in the stubborn logic of technology, nothing is quite real that cannot be stated in terms of tangible performance; and they are accordingly coming to understand that the whole fabric of credit and corporation finance is a tissue of make-believe.

Credit obligations and financial transactions rest on certain principles of legal formality which have been handed down from the eighteenth century, and which therefore antedate the mechanical industry and carry no secure conviction to men trained in the logic of that industry. Within this technological system of tangible performance corporation finance and all its works and gestures are completely idle; it all comes into the working scheme of the engineers only as a gratuitous intrusion which could be barred out without deranging the work at any point, provided only that men made up their mind to that effect—that is to say, provided the make-believe of absentee ownership were discontinued. Its only obvious effect on the work which the engineers have to take care of is waste of materials and retardation of the work. So the next question which the engineers are due to ask regarding this timeworn fabric of ownership, finance, sabotage, credit, and unearned income is likely to be: Why cumbers it the ground? And they are likely to find the scriptural answer ready to their hand.

It would be hazardous to surmise how, how soon, on what provocation, and with what effect the guild of engineers are due to realize that they constitute a guild, and that the material fortunes of the civilized peoples already lie loose in their hands. But it is already sufficiently plain that the industrial conditions and the drift of conviction among the engineers are drawing together to some such end.

Hitherto it has been usual to count on the interested negotiations continually carried on and never concluded between capital and labor, between the agents of the investors and the body of workmen, to bring about whatever readjustments are to be looked for in the control of productive industry and in the distribution and use of its product. These negotiations have necessarily been, and continue to be, in the nature of business transactions, bargaining for a price, since both parties to the negotiation continue to stand on the consecrated ground of ownership, free bargain, and self-help; such as the commercial wisdom of the eighteenth century saw, approved and certified it all, in the time before the coming of this perplexing industrial system. In the course of these endless negotiations betwen the owners and their workmen there has been some loose and provisional syndication of claims and forces on both sides; so that each of these two recognized parties to the industrial controversy has come to make up a loose-knit vested interest, and each speaks for its own special claims as a party in interest. Each is contending for some special gain for itself and trying to drive a profitable bargain for itself, and hitherto no disinterested spokesman for the community at large or for the industrial system as a going concern has seriously cut into this controversy between these contending vested interests. The outcome has been businesslike concession and compromise, in the nature of bargain and sale. It is true, during the war, and for the conduct of the war, there were some half-concerted measures taken by the Administration in the interest of the nation at large, as a belligerent; but it has always been tacitly agreed that these were extraordinary war measures, not to be countenanced in time of peace. In time of peace the accepted rule is still business as usual; that is to say, investors and workmen wrangling together on a footing of business as usual.

These negotiations have necessarily been inconclusive. So long as ownership of resources and industrial plant is allowed, or so long as it is allowed any degree of control or consideration in the conduct of industry, nothing more substantial can come of any readjustment than a concessive mitigation of the owners' interference with production. There is accordingly nothing subversive in these bouts of bargaining between the federated workmen and the syndicated owners. It is a game of chance and skill played between two contending vested interests for private gain, in which the industrial system as a going concern enters only as a victim of interested interference. Yet the material welfare of the community, and not least of the workmen, turns on the due working of this industrial system, without interference. Concessive mitigation of the right to interfere with production, on the part of either one of these vested interests, can evidently come to nothing more substantial than a concessive mitigation.

But owing to the peculiar technological character of this industrial system, with its specialized, standardized, mechanical, and highly technical interlocking processes of production, there has gradually come into being this corps of technological production specialists, into whose keeping the due functioning of the industrial system has now drifted by force of circumstance. They are, by force of circumstance, the keepers of the community's material welfare; although they have hitherto been acting, in effect, as keepers and pro-

viders of free income for the kept classes. They are thrown
into the position of responsible directors of the industrial
system, and by the same move they are in a position to become arbiters of the community's material welfare. They are
becoming class-conscious, and they are no longer driven by
a commercial interest, in any such degree as will make them
a vested interest in that commercial sense in which the syndicated owners and the federated workmen are vested interests. They are, at the same time, numerically and by
habitual outlook, no such heterogeneous and unwieldy body
as the federated workmen, whose numbers and scattering interest has left all their endeavors substantially nugatory. In
short, the engineers are in a position to make the next move.

By comparison with the population at large, including
the financial powers and the kept classes, the technological
specialists which come in question here are a very incon-
siderable number; yet this small number is indispensable to
the continued working of the productive industries. So slight
are their numbers, and so sharply defined and homogeneous
is their class, that a sufficiently compact and inclusive organization of their forces should arrange itself almost as a
matter of course, so soon as any appreciable proportion of
them shall be moved by any common purpose. And the common purpose is not far to seek, in the all-pervading industrial
confusion, obstruction, waste, and retardation which business as usual continually throws in their face. At the same
time they are leaders of the industrial personnel, the workmen, of the officers of the line and the rank and file; and these
are coming into a frame of mind to follow their leaders in
any adventure that holds a promise of advancing the common good.

To these men, soberly trained in a spirit of tangible performance and endowed with something more than an even
share of the sense of workmanship, and endowed also with
the common heritage of partiality for the rule of Live and
Let Live, the disallowance of an outworn and obstructive

right of absentee ownership is not likely to seem a shocking infraction of the sacred realities. That customary right of ownership by virtue of which the vested interests continue to control the industrial system for the benefit of the kept classes, belongs to an older order of things than the mechanical industry. It has come out of a past that was made up of small things and traditional make-believe. For all the purposes of that scheme of tangible performance that goes to make up the technologist's world, it is without form and void. So that, given time for due irritation, it should by no means come as a surprise if the guild of engineers are provoked to put their heads together and, quite out of hand, disallow that large absentee ownership that goes to make the vested interests and to unmake the industrial system. And there stand behind them the massed and rough-handed legions of the industrial rank and file, ill at ease and looking for new things. The older commercialized generation among them would, of course, ask themselves: Why should we worry? What do we stand to gain? But the younger generation, not so hard-bitten by commercial experience, will be quite as likely to ask themselves: What do we stand to lose? And there is the patent fact that such a thing as a general strike of the technological specialists in industry need involve no more than a minute fraction of one per cent. of the population; yet it would swiftly bring a collapse of the old order and sweep the timeworn fabric of finance and absentee sabotage into the discard for good and all.

Such a catastrophe would doubtless be deplorable. It would look something like the end of the world to all those persons who take their stand with the kept classes, but it may come to seem no more than an incident of the day's work to the engineers and to the rough-handed legions of the rank and file. It is a situation which may well be deplored. But there is no gain in losing patience with a conjunction of circumstances. And it can do no harm to take stock of the situation and recognize that, by force of circumstance, it is now open to the Council of Technological Workers' and Soldiers' Deputies to make the next move, in their own way and in their own good time. When and what this move will be, if any, or even what it will be like, is not something on which a layman can hold a confident opinion. But so much seems clear, that the industrial dictatorship of the captain of finance is now held on sufferance of the engineers and is liable at any time to be discontinued at their discretion, as a matter of convenience.

IV

*On the Danger
of a Revolutionary
Overturn*

Bolshevism is a menace to the vested rights of property and privilege. Therefore the guardians of the Vested Interests have been thrown into a state of Red trepidation by the continued functioning of Soviet Russia and the continual outbreaks of the same Red distemper elsewhere on the continent of Europe. It is feared, with a nerve-shattering fear, that the same Red distemper of Bolshevism must presently infect the underlying population in America and bring on an overturn of the established order, so soon as the underlying population are in a position to take stock of the situation and make up their mind to a course of action. The situation is an uneasy one, and it contains the elements of much trouble; at least such appears to be the conviction of the Guardians of the established order. Something of the kind is felt to be due, on the grounds of the accomplished facts. So it is feared, with a nerve-shattering fear, that anything like uncolored information as to the facts in the case and anything like a free popular discussion of these facts must logically result in disaster. Hence all this unseemly trepidation.

The Guardians of the Vested Interests, official and quasi-official, have allowed their own knowledge of this sinister state of things to unseat their common sense. The run of the facts has jostled them out of the ruts, and they have gone in for a headlong policy of clamor and repression, to cover and suppress matters of fact and to shut off discussion and deliberation. And all the while the Guardians are also feverishly at work on a mobilization of such forces as may hopefully be counted on to "keep the situation in hand" in case the expected should happen. The one manifestly conclusive resolution to which the Guardians of the Vested Interests have come is that the underlying population is to be "kept in hand," in the face of any contingency. Their one settled principle of conduct appears to be, to stick at nothing; in all of which, doubtless, the Guardians mean well.

Now, the Guardians of the Vested Interests are presumably wise in dicountenancing any open discussion or any free communication of ideas and opinions. It could lead to nothing more comfortable than popular irritation and distrust. The Vested Interests are known to have been actively concerned in the prosecution of the War, and there is no lack of evidence that their spokesmen have been heard in the subsequent counsels of the Peace. And, no doubt, the less that is known and said about the doings of the Vested Interests during the War and after, the better both for the public tranquility and for the continued growth and profit of the Vested Interests. Yet it is not to be overlooked that facts of such magnitude and of such urgent public concern as the manœuvres of the Vested Interests during the War and after can not be altogether happily covered over with a conspiracy of silence. Something like a middle course of temperate publicity should have seemed more to the point. It may be unfortunate, but it is none the less unavoidable, that something appreciable is bound to come to light; that is to say, something sinister.

It should be plain to all good citizens who have the cause of law and order at heart that in such a case a more genial policy of conciliatory promises and procrastination will be more to the purpose than any noisy recourse to the strong arm and the Star Chamber. A touch of history, and more particularly of contemporary history, would have given the Guardians a touch of sanity. Grown wise in all the ways and means of blamelessly defeating the unblest majority, the gentlemanly government of the British manage affairs of this kind much better. They have learned that bellicose gestures provoke ill will, and that desperate remedies should be held in reserve until needed. Whereas the Guardians of the Vested Interests in America are plainly putting things in train for a capital operation, for which there is no apparent necessity. It should be evident on slight reflection that things have not reached that fateful stage where nothing short of a capital operation can be counted on to save the life of the Vested Interests in America; not yet. And indeed, things need assuredly not reach such a stage if reasonable measures are taken to avoid undue alarm and irritation. All that is needed to keep the underlying population of America in a sweet temper is a degree of patient ambiguity and delay, something after the British pattern; and all will yet be well with the vested rights of property and privilege, for some time to come.

History teaches that no effectual popular uprising can be set afoot against an outworn institutional iniquity unless the movement effectually meets the special material requirements of the situation which provokes it; nor on the other hand can an impending popular overturn be staved off without making up one's account with those material conditions which converge to bring it on. The long history of British gentlemanly compromise, collusion, conciliation, and popular defeat, is highly instructive on that head. And it should be evident to any disinterested person, on any slight survey of the pertinent facts, that the situation in America does not now offer such a combination of circumstances as would be required for any effectual overturn of the established order or any forcible dispossession of these Vested Interests that now control the material fortunes of the American people. In short, by force of circumstances, Bolshevism is not a present menace to the Vested Interests in America; provided always that the Guardians of these Vested Interests do not go out of their way to precipitate trouble by such measures as will make Bolshevism of any complexion seem the lesser evil,—which is perhaps not a safe proviso, in view of the hysterically Red state of mind of the Guardians.

No movement for the dispossession of the Vested Interests in America can hope for even a temporary success unless it is undertaken by an organization which is competent to take over the country's productive industry as a whole, and to administer it from the start on a more efficient plan than that now pursued by the Vested Interests; and there is no such organization in sight or in immediate prospect. The nearest approach to a practicable organization of industrial forces in America, just yet, is the A. F. or L.; which need only be named in order to dispel the illusion that there is anything to hope or fear in the way of a radical move at its hands. The A. F. of L. is itself one of the Vested Interests, as ready as any other to do battle for its own margin of privilege and profit. At the same time it would be a wholly chimerical fancy to believe that such an organization of workmen as the A. F. of L. could take over and manage any appreciable section of the industrial system, even if their single-minded interest in special privileges for themselves did not preclude their making a move in that direction. The Federation is not organized for production but for bargaining. It is not organized on lines that would be workable for the management of any industrial system as a whole, or of any special line of production within such a system. It is, in effect, an organization for the strategic defeat of employers and rival organizations, by recourse to enforced unemployment and obstruction; not for the production of goods and services. And it is officered by tacticians, skilled in the ways and means of bargaining with politicians and intimidating employers and employees; not by men who have any special insight into or interest in the ways and means of quantity production and traffic management. They are not, and for their purpose they need not be, technicians in any conclusive sense,—and the fact should not be lost sight of that any effectual overturn, of the kind hazily contemplated by the hysterical officials, will always have to be primarily a technical affair.

In effect, the Federation is officered by safe and sane politicians, and its rank and file are votaries of "the full dinner-pail." No Guardian need worry about the Federation, and there is no other organization in sight which differs materially from the Federation in those respects which would count toward a practical move in the direction of a popular overturn,—unless a doubtful exception should be claimed for the Railroad Brotherhoods. The A. F. of L. is a business organization with a vested interest of its own; for keeping up prices and keeping down the supply, quite after the usual fashion of management by the other Vested Interests; not for managing productive industry or even for increasing the output of goods produced under any management. At the best, its purpose and ordinary business is to gain a little something for its own members at a more than proportionate cost to the rest of the community; which does not afford either the spiritual or the material ground for a popular overturn.

Nor is it the A. F. of L. or the other organizations for "collective bargaining" that come in for the comfortless attentions of the officials and of the many semi-official conspiracies in restraint of sobriety. Their nerve-shattering fears center rather on those irresponsible wayfaring men of industry who make up the I. W. W., and on the helpless and hapless alien unbelievers whose contribution to the sum total is loose talk in some foreign tongue. But if there is any assertion to be made without fear of stumbling it will be that this flotsam of industry is not organized to take over the highly technical duties involved in the administration of the industrial system. But it is these and their like that engage the best attention of the many commissions, committees, clubs, leagues, federations, syndicates, and corporations for the chasing of wild geese under the Red flag.

Wherever the mechanical industry has taken decisive effect, as in America and in the two or three industrialized regions of Europe, the community lives from hand to mouth in such a way that its livelihood depends on the effectual working of its industrial system from day to day. In such a case a serious disturbance and derangement of the balanced process of production is always easily brought on, and it always brings immediate hardship on large sections of the community. Indeed, it is this state of things—the ease with which industry can be deranged and hardship can be brought to bear on the people at large—that constitutes the chief asset of such partisan organizations as the A. F. of L. It is a state of things which makes sabotage easy and effectual and gives it breadth and scope. But sabotage is not revolution. If it were, then the A. F. of L., the I. W. W., the Chicago Packers, and the U. S. Senate would be counted among the revolutionists.

Far-reaching sabotage, that is to say derangement of the industrial system, such as to entail hardship on the community at large or on some particular section of it, is easily brought to bear in any country that is dominated by the mechanical industry. It is commonly resorted to by both parties in any controversy between the businesslike employers and the employees. It is, in fact, an everyday expedient of business, and no serious blame attaches to its ordinary use. Under given circumstances, as, e.g., under the circumstances just now created by the return of peace, such derangement of industry and hindrance of production is an unavoidable expedient of "business as usual." And derangement of the same nature is also commonly resorted to as a means of coercion in any attempted movement of overturn. It is the simple and obvious means of initiating any revolutionary disturbance in any industrial or commercialized country. But under the existing industrial conditions, if it is to achieve even a transient success, any such revolutionary movement of reconstruction must also be in a position from the outset to overcome any degree of initial derangement in industry, whether of its own making or not, and to do constructive work of that particular kind which is called for by the present disposition of industrial forces and by the present close dependence of the community's livelihood on the due systematic working of these industrial forces. To take effect and to hold its own even for the time being, any movement of overturn must from beforehand provide for a sufficiently productive conduct of the industrial system on which the community's material welfare depends, and for a competent distribution of goods and services throughout the community. Otherwise, under existing industrial conditions, nothing more can be accomplished than an ephemeral disturbance and a transient season of accentuated hardship. Even a transient failure to make good in the management of the industrial system must immediately defeat any movement of overturn in any of the advanced industrial countries. At this point the lessons of history fail, because the present industrial system and the manner of close-knit community life enforced by this industrial system have no example in history.

This state of things, which so conditions the possibility of any revolutionary overturn, is peculiar to the advanced industrial countries; and the limitations which this state of things imposes are binding within these countries in the same measure in which these peoples are dominated by the system of mechanical industry. In contrast with this state of things, the case of Soviet Russia may be cited to show the difference. As compared with America and much of western Europe, Russia is not an industrialized region, in any decisive sense; although Russia, too, leans on the mechanical industry in a greater degree than is commonly recognized. Indeed, so considerable is the dependence of the Russians on the mechanical industry that it may yet prove to be the decisive factor in the struggle which is now going on between Soviet Russia and the Allied Powers.

Now, it is doubtless this continued success of the Soviet

administration in Russia that has thrown this ecstatic scare into the Guardians of the Vested Interests in America and in the civilized countries of Europe. There is nothing to be gained by denying that the Russian Soviet has achieved a measure of success; indeed, an astonishing measure of success, considering the extremely adverse circumstances under which the Soviet has been at work. The fact may be deplored, but there it is. The Soviet has plainly been successful, in the material respect, far beyond the reports which have been allowed to pass the scrutiny of the Seven Censors and the Associated Prevarication Bureaux of the Allied Powers. And this continued success of Bolshevism in Russia—or such measure of success as it has achieved—is doubtless good ground for a reasonable degree of apprehension among good citizens elsewhere; but it does not by any means argue that anything like the same measure of success could be achieved by a revolutionary movement on the same lines in America, even in the absence of intervention from outside.

Soviet Russia has made good to the extent of maintaining itself against very great odds for some two years; and it is even yet a point in doubt whether the Allied Powers will be able to put down the Soviet by use of all the forces at their disposal and with the help of all the reactionary elements in Russia and in the neighboring countries. But the Soviet owes this measure of success to the fact that the Russian people have not yet been industrialized in anything like the same degree as their western neighbors. They have in great measure been able to fall back on an earlier, simpler, less close-knit plan of productive industry; such that any detailed part of this loose-knit Russian community is able, at a pinch, to draw its own livelihood from its own soil by its own work, without that instant and unremitting dependence on materials and wrought goods drawn from foreign ports and distant regions, that is characteristic of the advanced industrial peoples. This old-fashioned plan of home production does not involve an "industrial system" in the same exacting sense as the mechanical industry. The Russian industrial system, it is true, also runs on something of a balanced plan of give and take; it leans on the mechanical industry in some considerable degree and draws on foreign trade for many of its necessary articles of use; but for the transient time being, and for an appreciable interval of time, such a home-bred industrious population, living close to the soil and supplying its ordinary needs by home-bred handicraft methods, will be able to maintain itself in a fair state of efficiency if not in comfort, even in virtual isolation from the more advanced industrial centers and from the remoter sources of raw materials. To the ignorant,—that is to say, to the wise-acres of commerce,—this ability of the Russian people to continue alive and active under the conditions of an exemplary blockade has been a source of incredulous astonishment.

It is only as a fighting power, and then only for the purposes of an aggressive war, that such a community can count for virtually nothing in a contest with the advanced industrial nations. Such a people makes an unwieldy country to conquer from the outside. Soviet Russia is self-supporting, in a loose and comfortless way, and in this sense it is a very defensible country and may yet prove extremely difficult for the Allied Powers to subdue; but in the nature of the case there need be not the slightest shadow of apprehension that Soviet Russia can successfully take the offensive against any outside people, great or small, which has the use of the advanced mechanical industry.

The statesmen of the Allied Powers, who are now carrying on a covert war against Soviet Russia, are in a position to know this state of the case; and not least those American statesmen, who have by popular sentiment been constrained reluctantly to limit and mask their cooperation with the reactionary forces in Finland, Poland, the Ukraine, Siberia, and elsewhere. They have all been at pains diligently to inquire into the state of things in Soviet Russia; although, it is true, they have also been at pains to give out surprisingly little information,—that being much of the reason for the Seven Censors. The well-published official and semi-official apprehension of a Bolshevist offensive to be carried on beyond the Soviet frontiers may quite safely be set down as an article of statesmanlike subterfuge. The statesmen know better. What is feared in fact is infection of the Bolshevist spirit beyond the Soviet frontiers, to the detriment of those Vested Interests whose guardians these statesmen are. And on this head the apprehensions of these Elder Statesmen are not altogether groundless; for the Elder Statesmen are also in a position to know, without much inquiry, that there is no single spot or corner in civilized Europe or America where the underlying population would have anything to lose by such an overturn of the established order as would cancel the vested rights of privilege and property, whose guardians they are.

But commercialized America is not the same thing as Soviet Russia. By and large, America is an advanced industrial country, bound in the web of a fairly close-knit and inclusive industrial system. The industrial situation, and therefore the conditions of success, are radically different in the two countries in those respects that would make the outcome in any effectual revolt. So that, for better or worse, the main lines that would necessarily have to be followed in working out any practicable revolutionary movement in this country are already laid down by the material conditions of its productive industry. On provocation there might come a flare of riotous disorder; but it would come to nothing, however substantial the provocation might be, so long as the movement does not fall in with those main lines of management which the state of the industrial system requires in order to insure any sustained success. These main lines of revolutionary strategy are lines of technical organization and industrial management; essentially lines of industrial engineering; such as will fit the organization to take care of the highly technical industrial system that constitutes the indispensable material foundation of any modern civilized community. They will accordingly not only be of a profoundly different order from what may do well enough in the case of such a loose-knit and backward industrial region as Russia, but they will necessarily also be of a kind which has no close parallel in the past history of revolutionary movements. Revolutions in the eighteenth century were military and political; and the Elder Statesmen who now believe themselves to be making history still believe that revolutions can be made and unmade by the same ways and means in the twentieth century. But any substantial or effectual overturn in the twentieth century will necessarily be an industrial overturn; and by the same token, any twentieth-century revolution can be combated or neutralized only by industrial ways and means. The case of America, therefore, considered as a candidate for Bolshevism, will have to be argued on its own merits, and the argument will necessarily turn on the ways and means of productive industry as conditioned by the later growth of technology.

It has been argued, and it seems not unreasonable to believe, that the established order of business enterprise, vested rights, and commercialized nationalism, is due presently to go under in a muddle of shame and confusion, because it is no longer a practicable system of industrial management under the conditions created by the later state of the industrial arts. Twentieth-century technology has outgrown the eighteenth-century system of vested rights. The experience of the past few years teaches that the usual management of industry by business methods has become highly inefficient and wasteful, and the indications are many and obvious that any businesslike control of production and distribution is bound to run more and more consistently at cross purposes with the community's livelihood, the farther the industrial arts advance and the wider the industrial system extends. So that it is perhaps not reasonably to be questioned that Vested Interests in business are riding for a fall. But the end is not yet; although it is to be admitted, regretfully perhaps, that with every further advance in technological knowledge and practice and with every further increase in the volume and complexity of the industrial system, any businesslike control is bound to grow still more incompetent, irrelevant, and impertinent.

It would be quite hazardous to guess, just yet, how far off that consummation of commercial imbecility may be. There are those who argue that the existing system of business management is plainly due to go under within two years' time; and there are others who are ready, with equal confidence, to allow it a probable duration of several times that interval; although, it is true, these latter appear, on the whole, to be persons who are less intimately acquainted with the facts in the case. Many men experienced in the larger affairs of industrial business are in doubt as to how long things will hold together. But, one with another, these men who so are looking into the doubtful future are, somewhat apprehensively, willing to admit that there is yet something of a margin to go on; so much so that, barring accident, there should seem to be no warrant for counting at all confidently on a disastrous breakdown of the business system within anything like a two-year period. And, for the reassurance of the apprehensive Guardian of the Vested Interests, it is to be added that should such a break in the situation come while things are standing in their present shape, the outcome could assuredly not be an effectual overturn of the established order; so long as no practicable plan has been provided for taking over the management from the dead hand of the Vested Interests. Should such a self-made breakdown come at the present juncture, the outcome could, in fact, scarcely be anything more serious than an interval, essentially transient though more or less protracted, of turmoil and famine among the underlying population, together with something of a setback to the industrial system as a whole. There seems no reason to apprehend any substantial disallowance of the vested rights of property to follow from such an essentially ephemeral interlude of dissension. In fact, the tenure of the Vested Interests in America should seem to be reasonably secure, just yet.

Something in the nature of riotous discontent and factional disorder is perhaps to be looked for in the near future in this country, and there may even be some rash gesture of revolt on the part of ill-advised malcontents. Circumstances would seem to favor something of the kind. It is conservatively estimated that there is already a season of privation and uncertainty in prospect for the underlying population, which could be averted only at the cost of some substantial interference with the vested rights of the country's business men,—which should seem a highly improbable alternative, in view of that spirit of filial piety with which the public officials guard the prerogatives of business as usual. So, e.g., it is now (September, 1919) confidently expected, or rather computed, that a fuel famine is due in America during the approaching winter, for reasons of sound business management; and it is likewise to be expected that for the like reason the American transportation system is also due to go into a tangle of congestion and idleness about the same time—barring providential intervention in the way of unexampled weather conditions. But a season of famine and disorderly conduct does not constitute a revolutionary overturn of the established order; and the Vested Interests are secure in their continued usufruct of the country's industry, just yet.

This hopeful posture of things may be shown convincingly enough and with no great expenditure of argument. To this end it is proposed to pursue the argument somewhat further presently by describing in outline what are the infirmities of the régime of the Vested Interests, which the more sanguine malcontents count on to bring that régime to an inglorious finish in the immediate future; and also to set down, likewise in outline, what would have to be the character of any organization of industrial forces which could be counted on effectually to wind up the régime of the Vested Interests and take over the management of the industrial system on a deliberate plan.

V

On the Circumstances Which Make for a Change

The state of industry, in America and in the other advanced industrial countries, will impose certain exacting conditions on any movement that aims to displace the Vested Interests. These conditions lie in the nature of things; that is to say, in the nature of the existing industrial system; and until they are met in some passable fashion, this industrial system can not be taken over in any effectual or enduring manner. And it is plain that whatever is found to be true in these respects for America will also hold true in much the same degree for the other countries that are dominated by the mechanical industry and the system of absentee ownership.

It may also confidently be set down at the outset that such an impartial review of the evidence as is here aimed at will make it appear that there need be no present apprehension of the Vested Interests' being unseated by any popular uprising in America, even if the popular irritation should rise very appreciably above its present pitch, and even if certain advocates of "direct action," here and there, should be so ill-advised as to make some rash gesture of revolt. The only present danger is that a boisterous campaign of repression and inquisition on the part of the Guardians of the Vested Interests may stir up some transient flutter of seditious disturbance.

To this end, then, it will be necessary to recall, in a summary way, those main facts of the industrial system and of the present businesslike control of this system which come immediately into the case. By way of general premise it is to be noted that the established order of business rests on absentee ownership and is managed with an eye single to the largest obtainable net return in terms of price; that is to say, it is a system of businesslike management on a commercial footing. The underlying population is dependent on the working of this industrial system for its livelihood; and their material interest therefore centers in the output and distribution of consumable goods, not in an increasing volume of earnings for the absentee owners. Hence there is a division of interest between the business community, who do business for the absentee owners, and the underlying population, who work for a living; and in the nature of the case this division of interest between the absentee owners and the underlying population is growing wider and more evident from day to day; which engenders a certain division of sentiment and a degree of mutual distrust. With it all the underlying population are still in a sufficiently deferential frame of mind toward their absentee owners, and are quite conscientiously delicate about any abatement of the free income which their owners come in for, according to the rules of the game as it is played.

The business concerns which so have the management of industry on this plan of absentee ownership are capitalized on their business capacity, not on their industrial capacity; that is to say, they are capitalized on their capacity to produce earnings, not on their capacity to produce goods. Their capitalization has, in effect, been calculated and fixed on the highest ordinary rate of earnings previously obtained; and on pain of insolvency their businesslike managers are now required to meet fixed income-charges on this capitalization. Therefore, as a proposition of safe and sane business management, prices have to be maintained or advanced.

From this businesslike requirement of meeting these fixed overhead charges on the capitalization there result certain customary lines of waste and obstruction, which are unavoidable so long as industry is managed by businesslike methods and for businesslike ends. These ordinary lines of waste and obstruction are necessarily (and blamelessly) included in the businesslike conduct of production. They are many and various in detail, but they may for convenience be classed under four heads: (a) Unemployment of material resources, equipment and manpower, in whole or in part, deliberately or through ignorance; (b) Salesmanship (includes, e.g., needless multiplication of merchants and shops, wholesale and retail, newspaper advertising and bill-boards, sales-exhibits, sales-agents, fancy packages and labels, adulteration, multiplication of brands and proprietary articles); (c) Production (and sales-cost) of superfluities and spurious goods; (d) Systematic dislocation, sabotage and duplication, due in part to businesslike strategy, in part to businesslike ignorance of industrial requirements (includes, e.g., such things as cross-freights, monopolization of resources, withholding of facilities and information from business rivals whom it is thought wise to hinder or defeat). There is, of course, no blame, and no sense of blame or shame attaching to all this everyday waste and confusion that goes to make up the workday total of businesslike management. All of it is a legitimate and necessary part of the established order of business enterprise, within the law and within the ethics of the trade.

Salesmanship is the most conspicuous, and perhaps the gravest, of these wasteful and industrially futile practices that are involved in the businesslike conduct of industry; it bulks large both in its immediate cost and in its meretricious consequences. It also is altogether legitimate and indispensable in any industrial business that deals with customers, in buying or selling; which comes near saying, in all business that has to do with the production or distribution of goods or services. Indeed, salesmanship is, in a way, the whole end and substance of business enterprise; and except so far as it is managed with a constant view to profitable bargains, the production of goods is not a business proposition. It is the elimination of profitable transactions of purchase and sale that is hoped for by any current movement looking to an overturn; and it is the same elimination of profitable bargaining that is feared, with a nerve-shattering fear, by the Guardians of the established order. Salesmanship is also the most indispensable and most meritorious of those qualities that go to make a safe and sane business man.

It is doubtless within the mark to say that, at an average, one-half the price paid for goods and services by consumers is to be set down to the account of salesmanship—that is, to sales-cost and to the net gains of salesmanship. But in many notable lines of merchandise the sales-cost will ordinarily foot up to some ten or twenty times the production-cost proper, and to not less than one hundred times the necessary cost of distribution. All this is not a matter for shame or distaste. In fact, just now more than ever, there is a clamorous and visibly growing insistence on the paramount merit and importance of salesmanship as the main stay of commerce and industry, and a strenuous demand for more extensive and more thorough training in salesmanship of a larger number of young men—at the public expense—to enable a shrewdly limited output of goods to be sold at more profitable prices— at the public cost. So also there is a visibly increasing expenditure on all manner of advertising; and the spokesmen of this enterprise in conspicuous waste are "pointing with pride" to the fact that the American business community have already spent upward of $600,000,000 on bill-boards alone within the past year, not to speak of much larger sums spent on newspapers and other printed matter for the same purpose —and the common man pays the cost.

At the same time advertising and manœuvres of salesmanlike spell-binding appear to be the only resource to which the country's business men know how to turn for relief from that tangle of difficulties into which the outbreak of a businesslike peace has precipitated the commercialized world. Increased sales-cost is to remedy the evils of under-production. In this connection it may be worth while to recall, without heat or faultfinding, that all the costly publicity that goes into sales-costs is in the nature of prevarication, when it is not good broad mendacity; and quite necessarily so. And all the while the proportion of sales-costs to production-costs goes on increasing, and the cost of living grows continually greater for the underlying population, and business necessities continue to enlarge the necessary expenditure on ways and means of salesmanship.

It is reasonable to believe that this state of things, which has been coming on gradually for some time past, will in time come to be understood and appreciated by the underlying population, at least in some degree. And it is likewise reasonable to believe that so soon as the underlying population come to realize that all this wasteful traffic of salesmanship is using up their productive forces, with nothing better to show for it than an increased cost of living, they will be driven to make some move to abate the nuisance. And just so far as this state of things is now beginning to be understood, its logical outcome is a growing distrust of the business men and all their works and words. But the underlying population is still very credulous about anything that is said or done in the name of Business, and there need be no apprehension of a mutinous outbreak, just yet. But at the same time it is evident that any plan of management which could contrive to dispense with all this expenditure on salesmanship, or that could materially reduce sales-costs, would have that much of a free margin to go on, and therefore that much of an added chance of success; and so also it is evident that any other than a business-like management could so contrive, inasmuch as sales-costs are incurred solely for purposes of business, not for purposes of industry; they are incurred for the sake of private gain, not for the sake of productive work.

But there is in fact no present promise of a breakdown of business, due to the continued increase of sales-costs; although sales-costs are bound to go on increasing so long as the country's industry continues to be managed on anything like the present plan. In fact, salesmanship is the chief factor in that ever-increasing cost of living, which is in its turn the chief ground of prosperity among the business community and the chief source of perennial hardship and discontent among the underlying population. Still it is worth noting that the eventual elimination of salesmanship and sales-cost would lighten the burden of workday production for the underlying population by some fifty per cent. There is that much of a visible inducement to disallow that system of absentee owner-ship on which modern business enterprise rests; and—for what it may be worth—it is to be admitted that there is there-fore that much of a drift in the existing state of things toward a revolutionary overturn looking to the unseating of the Vested Interests. But at the same time the elimination of salesmanship and all its voluminous apparatus and traffic would also cut down the capitalized income of the business community by something like one-half; and that contingency is not to be contemplated, not to say with equanimity, by the Guardians; and it is after all in the hands of these Guardians that the fortunes of the community rest. Such a move is a moral impossibility, just yet.

Closely related to the wasteful practices of salesmanship as commonly understood, if it should not rather be counted in as an extension of salesmanship, is that persistent unem-ployment of men, equipment, and material resources, by which the output of goods and services is kept down to the "requirements of the market," with a view to maintaining prices at a "reasonably profitable level." Such unemployment, deliberate and habitual, is one of the ordinary expedients em-ployed in the businesslike management of industry. There is always more or less of it in ordinary times. "Reasonable earnings" could not be assured without it; because "what the traffic will bear" in the way of an output of goods is by no means the same as the productive capacity of the industrial system; still less is it the same as the total consumptive needs of the community; in fact, it does not visibly tend to coincide with either. It is more particularly in times of popular distress, such as the present year, when the current output of goods is not nearly sufficient to cover the consumptive needs of the community, that considerations of business strategy call for a wise unemployment of the country's productive forces. At the same time, such businesslike unemployment of equipment and man power is the most obvious cause of popular distress.

All this is well known to the Guardians of the Vested Interests, and their knowledge of it is, quite reasonably, a source of uneasiness to them. But they see no help for it; and indeed there is no help for it within the framework of "business as usual," since it is the essence of business as usual. So also, the Guardians are aware that this businesslike sabotage on productive industry is a fruitful source of discontent and distrust among the underlying population who suffer the inconvenience of it all; and they are beset with the abiding fear that the underlying population may shortly be provoked into disallowing those Vested Interests for whose benefit this deliberate and habitual sabotage on production is carried on. It is felt that here again is a sufficient reason why the businesslike management of industry should be discontinued; which is the same as saying that here again is a visibly sufficient reason for such a revolutionary overturn as will close out the Old Order of absentee ownership and capitalized income. It is also evident that any plan which shall contrive to dispense with this deliberate and habitual unemployment of men and equipment will have that much more of a margin to go on, both in respect of practical efficiency and in respect of popular tolerance; and evidently, too, any other than a businesslike management of industry can so contrive, as a matter of course; inasmuch as any such unbusinesslike administration—as, e.g., the Soviet—will be relieved of the businesslike manager's blackest bug-bear, "a reasonably profitable level of prices."

But for all that, those shudderingly sanguine persons who are looking for a dissolution of the system of absentee ownership within two years' time are not counting on salesmanlike waste and businesslike sabotage to bring on the collapse, so much as they count on the item listed under (d) above—the systematic dislocation and all-round defeat of productive industry which is due in part to shrewd manœuvres of businesslike strategy, in part to the habitual ignorance of business men touching the systematic requirements of the industrial system as a whole. The shrewd worldly wisdom of the businesslike managers, looking consistently to the main chance, works in harmoniously with their trained ignorance on matters of technology, to bring about what amounts to effectual team-work for the defeat of the country's industrial system as a going concern. Yet doubtless this sinister hope of a collapse within two years is too sanguine. Doubtless the underlying population can be counted on stolidly to put up with what they are so well used to, just yet; more particularly so long as they are not in the habit of thinking about these things at all. Nor does it seem reasonable to believe that this all-pervading waste and confusion of industrial forces will of itself bring the business organization to a collapse within so short a time.

It is true, the industrial system is continually growing, in volume and complication; and with every new extension of its scope and range, and with every added increment of technological practice that goes into effect, there comes a new and urgent opportunity for the business men in control to extend and speed up their strategy of mutual obstruction and defeat; it is all in the day's work. As the industrial system grows larger and more closely interwoven it offers continually larger and more enticing opportunities for such businesslike manœuvres as will effectually derange the system at the same time that they bring the desired tactical defeat on some business rival; whereby the successful business strategist is enabled to get a little something for nothing at a constantly increasing cost to the community at large. With every increment of growth and maturity the country's industrial system becomes more delicately balanced, more intricately bound in a web of industrial give and take, more sensitive to far-reaching derangement by any local dislocation, more widely and instantly responsive to any failure of the due correlation at any point; and by the same move the captains of industry, to whose care the interests of absentee ownership are entrusted, are enabled, or rather they are driven by the necessities of competitive business, to plan their strategy of mutual defeat and derangement on larger and more intricate lines, with an ever wider reach and a more massive mobilization of forces. From which follows an ever increasing insecurity of work and output from day to day and an increased assurance of general loss and disability in the long run; incidentally coupled with increased hardship for the underlying population, which comes in all along as a subsidiary matter of course, unfortunate but unavoidable. It is this visibly growing failure of the present businesslike management to come up to the industrial necessities of the case; its unfitness to take anything like reasonable care of the needed correlation of industrial forces within the system; its continual working at cross purposes in the allocation of energy resources, materials, and man power—it is this fact, that any businesslike management of necessity runs at cross purposes with the larger technical realities of the industrial system, that chiefly goes to persuade apprehensive persons that the régime of business enterprise is fast approaching the limit of tolerance. So it is held by many that this existing system of absentee ownership must presently break down and precipitate the abdication of the Vested Interests, under conviction of total imbecility.

The theory on which these apprehensive persons proceed appears to be substantially sound, so far as it goes, but they reach an unguardedly desperate conclusion because they overlook one of the main facts of the case. There is no reasonable exception to be taken to the statement that the country's industrial system is forever growing more extensive and more complex; that it is continually taking on more of the character of a close-knit, interwoven, systematic whole; a delicately balanced moving equilibrium of working parts, no one of which can do its work by itself at all, and none of which can do its share of the work well except in close correlation with all the rest. At the same time it is also true that, in the commercialized nature of things, the businesslike management of industry is forever playing fast and loose with this delicately balanced moving equilibrium of forces, on which the livelihood of the underlying population depends from day to day; more particularly is this true for that large-scale business enterprise that rests on absentee ownership and makes up the country's greater Vested Interests. But to all this it is to be added, as a corrective and a main factor in the case, that this system of mechanical industry is an extremely efficient contrivance for the production of goods and services, even when, as usual, the business men, for business reasons, will allow it to work only under a large handicap of unemployment and obstructive tactics. Hitherto the margin for error, that is to say for wasteful strategy and obstructive ignorance, has been very wide; so wide that it has saved the life of the Vested Interests; and it is accordingly by no means confidently to be believed that all these ampler opportunities for swift and wide-reaching derangement will enable the strategy of business enterprise to bring on a disastrous collapse, just yet.

It is true, if the country's productive industry were competently organized as a systematic whole, and were then managed by competent technicians with an eye single to maximum production of goods and services; instead of, as now, being manhandled by ignorant business men with an

eye single to maximum profits; the resulting output of goods
and services would doubtless exceed the current output by
several hundred per cent. But then, none of all that is necessary to save the established order of things. All this is required is a decent modicum of efficiency, very far short of
the theoretical maximum production. In effect, the community is in the habit of getting along contentedly on something appreciably less than one-half the output which its
industrial equipment would turn out if it were working
uninterruptedly at full capacity; even when, as usual, something like one-half of the actual output is consumed in wasteful superfluities. The margin for waste and error is very wide,
fortunately; and, in effect, a more patient and more inclusive
survey of the facts in the case would suffice to show that the
tenure of the Vested Interests is reasonably secure just yet;
at least in so far as it turns on considerations of this nature.

There is, of course, the chance, and it is by no means
a remote chance, that the rapidly increasing volume and complexity of the industrial system may presently bring the
country's industry into such a ticklish state of unstable equilibrium that even a reasonable modicum of willful derangement can no longer be tolerated, even for the most urgent
and most legitimate reasons of businesslike strategy and
vested rights. In time, such an outcome is presumably due
to be looked for. There is, indeed, no lack of evidence that
the advanced industrial countries are approaching such a
state of things, America among the rest. The margin for
error and wasteful strategy is, in effect, being continually
narrowed by the further advance of the industrial arts. With
every further advance in the way of specialization and standardization, in point of kind, quantity, quality, and time, the
tolerance of the system as a whole under any strategic maladjustment grows continually narrower.

How soon the limit of tolerance for willful derangement
is due to be reached would be a hazardous topic of speculation. There is now a fair prospect that the coming winter

may throw some light on that dark question; but this is not saying that the end is in sight. What is here insisted on is that that sinister eventuality lies yet in the future, although it may be in the calculable future. So also it is well to keep in mind that even a fairly disastrous collapse of the existing system of businesslike management need by no means prove fatal to the Vested Interests, just yet; not so long as there is no competent organization ready to take their place and administer the country's industry on a more reasonable plan. It is necessarily a question of alternatives.

In all this argument that runs on perennial dislocation and cross purposes, it is assumed that the existing businesslike management of industry is of a competitive nature and necessarily moves on lines of competitive strategy. As a subsidiary premise it is, of course, also assumed that the captains of industry who have the direction of this competitive strategy are ordinarily sufficiently ill informed on technological matters to go wrong, industrially speaking, even with the most pacific and benevolent intentions. They are laymen in all that concerns the technical demands of industrial production. This latter, and minor, assumption therefore need not be argued; it is sufficiently notorious. On the other hand, the first assumption spoken of above, that current business enterprise is of a competitive nature, is likely to be questioned by many who believe themselves to be familiar with the facts in the case. It is argued, by one and another, that the country's business concerns have entered into consolidations, coalitions, understandings and working arrangements among themselves—syndicates, trusts, pools, combinations, interlocking directorates, gentlemen's agreements, employers' unions—to such an extent as virtually to cover the field of that large-scale business that sets the pace and governs the movements of the rest; and that where combination takes effect in this way, competition ceases. So also it will be argued that where there has been no formal coalition of interests the business men in charge will still commonly act in collusion, with much the same result. The suggestion is also ready to hand that in so far as businesslike sabotage of this competitive order is still to be met with, it can all be corrected by such a further consolidation of interests as will do away with all occasion for competitive cross purposes within the industrial system.

It is not easy to see just how far that line of argument would lead; but to make it effective and to cover the case it would plainly have to result in so wide a coalition of interests and pooling of management as would, in effect, eliminate all occasion for businesslike management within the system, and leave the underlying population quite unreservedly at the disposal of the resulting coalition of interests —an outcome which is presumably not contemplated. And even so, the argument takes account of only one strand in that three-ply rope that goes to fashion the fatal noose. The remaining two are stout enough, and they have not been touched. It is true, economists and others who have canvassed this matter of competition have commonly given their attention to this one line of competition alone—between rival commercial interests—because this competition is conceived to be natural and normal and to serve the common good. But there remains (a) the competition between those business men who buy cheap and sell dear and the underlying population from and to whom they buy cheap and sell dear, and (b) the competition between the captains of industry and those absentee owners in whose name and with whose funds the captains do business. In the typical case, modern business enterprise takes the corporate form, is organized on credit, and therefore rests on absentee ownership; from which it follows that in all large-scale business the owners are not the same persons as the managers, nor does the interest of the manager commonly coincide with that of his absentee owners, particularly in the modern "big business."

So it follows that even a coalition of Vested Interests

which should be virtually all-inclusive, would still have to make up its account with "what the traffic will bear," that is to say what will bring the largest net income in terms of price; that is to say, the coalition would still be under the competitive necessity of buying cheap and selling dear, to the best of its ability and with the use of all the facilities which its dominant position in the market would give. The coalition, therefore, would still be under the necessity of shrewdly limiting the output of goods and services to such a rate and volume as will maintain or advance prices; and also to vary its manipulation of prices and supply from place to place and from time to time, to turn an honest penny; which leaves the case very near the point of beginning. But then, such a remedy for these infelicities of the competitive system will probably be admitted to be chimerical, without argument.

But what is more to the point is the fact, known even when it is not avowed, that the consolidations which have been effected hitherto have not eliminated competition, nor have they changed the character of the competitive strategy employed, although they have altered its scale and methods. What can be said is that the underlying corporations of the holding companies, e.g., are no longer competitors among themselves on the ancient footing. But strategic dislocation and cross purposes continue to be the order of the day in the businesslike management of industry; and the volume of habitual unemployment, whether of equipment or of man power, continues undiminished and unashamed—which is after all a major count in the case.

It is well to recognize what the business men among themselves always recognize as a matter of course, that business is in the last analysis always carried on for the private advantage of the individual business men who carry it on. And these enterprising persons, being business men, will always be competitors for gain among themselves, however much and well they may combine for a common purpose as against the rest of the community. The end and aim of any gainful enterprise carried through in common is always the division of the joint gains, and in this division the joint participants always figure as competitors. The syndicates, coalitions, corporations, consolidations of interests, so entered into the pursuit of gain are, in effect, in the nature of conspiracies between business men each seeking his own advantage at the cost of any whom it may concern. There is no ulterior solidarity of interests among the participants in such a joint enterprise.

By way of illustration, what is set forth in the voluminous testimony taken in the Colton case, before the California courts, having to do with the affairs of the Southern Pacific and its subsidiaries, will show in what fashion the business-like incentives of associated individuals may be expected to work out in the partition of benefits within a given coalition. And not only is there no abiding solidarity of interests between the several participants in such a joint enterprise, so far as regards the final division of the spoils, but it is also true that the business interest of the manager in charge of such a syndicate of absentee ownership will not coincide with the collective interest of the coalition as a going concern. As an illustrative instance may be cited the testimony of the great president of the two Great Northern railways, taken before a Congressional commission, wherein it is explained somewhat fully that for something like a quarter-century the two great roads under his management had never come in for reasonable earnings on their invested capital. And it is a matter of common notoriety, although it was charitably not brought out in the hearings of the commission, that during his incumbency as manager of the two great railway systems this enterprising railway president had by thrift and management increased his own private possessions from $20 to something variously estimated at $150,000,000 to $200,000,000; while his two chief associates in this adventure had retired from the management on a similarly comfortable footing; so notably comfortable, indeed, as to have merited a couple of very decent peerages under the British crown.

In effect, there still is an open call for shrewd personal strategy at the cost of any whom it may concern; all the while that there is also a very appreciable measure of collusion among the Vested Interests, at the cost of any whom it may concern. Business is still competitive business, competitive pursuit of private gain; as how should it not be? seeing that the incentive to all business is after all private gain at the cost of any whom it may concern.

By reason of doctrinal consistency and loyalty to tradition, the certified economists have habitually described business enterprise as a rational arrangement for administering the country's industrial system and assuring a full and equitable distribution of consumable goods to the consumers. There need be no quarrel with that view. But it is only fair to enter the reservation that, considered as an arrangement for administering the country's industrial system, business enterprise based on absentee ownership has the defects of its qualities; and these defects of this good old plan are now calling attention to themselves. Hitherto, and ever since the mechanical industry first came into the dominant place in this industrial system, the defects of this businesslike management of industry have continually been encroaching more and more on its qualities. It took its rise as a system of management by the owners of the industrial equipment, and it has in its riper years grown into a system of absentee ownership managed by quasi-responsible financial agents. Having begun as an industrial community which centered about an open market, it has matured into a community of Vested Interests whose vested right it is to keep up prices by a short supply in a closed market. There is no extravagance in saying that, by and large, this arrangement for controlling the production and distribution of goods and services through the agency of absentee ownership has now come to be, in the main, a blundering muddle of defects. For the purpose in hand, that is to say with a view to the probable chance of any revolutionary overturn, this may serve as a fair characterization of the régime of the Vested Interests; whose continued rule is now believed by their Guardians to be threatened by a popular uprising in the nature of Bolshevism.

Now, as to the country's industrial system which is manhandled on this businesslike plan; it is a comprehensive and balanced scheme of technological administration. Industry of this modern sort—mechanical, specialized, standardized, running to quantity production, drawn on a large scale—is highly productive; provided always that the necessary conditions of its working are met in some passable fashion. These necessary conditions of productive industry are of a well-defined technical character, and they are growing more and more exacting with every farther advance in the industrial arts. This mechanical industry draws always more and more largely and urgently on the natural sources of mechanical power, and it necessarily makes use of an ever increasingly wide and varied range of materials, drawn from all latitudes and all geographical regions, in spite of obstructive national frontiers and patriotic animosities; for the mechanical technology is impersonal and dispassionate, and its end is very simply to serve human needs, without fear or favor or respect of persons, prerogatives, or politics. It makes up an industrial system of an unexampled character— a mechanically balanced and interlocking system of work to be done, the prime requisite of whose working is a painstaking and intelligent co-ordination of the processes at work, and an equally painstaking allocation of mechanical power and materials. The foundation and driving force of it all is a massive body by technological knowledge, of a highly impersonal and altogether unbusinesslike nature, running in close contact with the material sciences, on which it draws freely at every turn—exactingly specialized, endlessly detailed, reaching out into all domains of empirical fact.

Such is the system of productive work which has grown out of the Industrial Revolution, and on the full and free run of which the material welfare of all the civilized peoples now depends from day to day. Any defect or hindrance in its technical administration, any intrusion of non-technical considerations, any failure or obstruction at any point, unavoidably results in a disproportionate set-back to the balanced whole and brings a disproportionate burden of privation on all these peoples whose productive industry has come within the sweep of the system.

It follows that those gifted, trained, and experienced technicians who now are in possession of the requisite technological information and experience are the first and instantly indispensable factor in the everyday work of carrying on the country's productive industry. They now constitute the General Staff of the industrial system, in fact; whatever law and custom may formally say in protest. The "captains of industry" may still vaingloriously claim that distinction, and law and custom still countenance their claim; but the captains have no technological value, in fact.

Therefore any question of a revolutionary overturn, in America or in any other of the advanced industrial countries, resolves itself in practical fact into a question of what the guild of technicians will do. In effect it is a question whether the discretion and responsibility in the management of the country's industry shall pass from the financiers, who speak for the Vested Interests, to the technicians, who speak for the industrial system as a going concern. There is no third party qualified to make a colorable bid, or able to make good its pretensions if it should make a bid. So long as the vested rights of absentee ownership remain intact, the financial powers—that is to say the Vested Interests—will continue to dispose of the country's industrial forces for their own profit;

and so soon, or so far, as these vested rights give way, the control of the people's material welfare will pass into the hands of the technicians. There is no third party.

The chances of anything like a Soviet in America, therefore, are the chances of a Soviet of technicians. And, to the due comfort of the Guardians of the Vested Interests and the good citizens who make up their background, it can be shown that anything like a Soviet of Technicians is at the most a remote contingency in America.

It is true, so long as no such change of base is made, what is confidently to be looked for is a régime of continued and increasing shame and confusion, hardship and dissension, unemployment and privation, waste and insecurity of person and property—such as the rule of the Vested Interests in business has already made increasingly familiar to all the civilized peoples. But the vested rights of absentee ownership are still embedded in the sentiments of the underlying population, and still continue to be the Palladium of the Republic; and the assertion is still quite safe that anything like a Soviet of Technicians is not a present menace to the Vested Interests in America.

By settled habit the technicians, the engineers and industrial experts, are a harmless and docile sort, well fed on the whole, and somewhat placidly content with the "full dinner-pail" which the lieutenants of the Vested Interests habitually allow them. It is true, they constitute the indispensable General Staff of that industrial system which feeds the Vested Interests; but hitherto at least, they have had nothing to say in the planning and direction of this industrial system, except as employees in the pay of the financiers. They have, hitherto, been quite unreflectingly content to work piecemeal, without much of an understanding among themselves, unreservedly doing job-work for the Vested Interests; and they have without much reflection lent themselves and their technical powers freely to the obstructive tactics of the captains of industry; all the while that the training which makes them technicians is but a specialized extension of that joint stock of technological knowledge that has been carried forward out of the past by the community at large.

But it remains true that they and their dear-bought knowledge of ways and means—dear-bought on the part of the underlying community—are the pillars of that house of industry in which the Vested Interests continue to live. Without their continued and unremitting supervision and direction the industrial system would cease to be a working system at all; whereas it is not easy to see how the elimination of the existing businesslike control could bring anything but relief and heightened efficiency to this working system. The technicians are indispensable to productive industry of this mechanical sort; the Vested Interests and their absentee owners are not. The technicians are indispensable to the Vested Interests and their absentee owners, as a working force without which there would be no industrial output to control or divide; whereas the Vested Interests and their absentee owners are of no material consequence to the technicians and their work, except as an extraneous interference and obstruction.

It follows that the material welfare of all the advanced industrial peoples rests in the hands of these technicians, if they will only see it that way, take counsel together, constitute themselves the self-directing General Staff of the country's industry, and dispense with the interference of the lieutenants of the absentee owners. Already they are strategically in a position to take the lead and impose their own terms of leadership, so soon as they, or a decisive number of them, shall reach a common understanding to that effect and agree on a plan of action.

But there is assuredly no present promise of the technicians' turning their insight and common sense to such use. There need be no present apprehension. The technicians are a "safe and sane" lot, on the whole; and they are pretty well commercialized, particularly the older generation, who speak with authority and conviction, and to whom the younger generation of engineers defer, on the whole, with such a degree of filial piety as should go far to reassure all good citizens. And herein lies the present security of the Vested Interests, as well as the fatuity of any present alarm about Bolshevism and the like; for the whole-hearted co-operation of the technicians would be as indispensable to any effectual movement of overturn as their unwavering service in the employ of the Vested Interests is indispensable to the maintenance of the established order.

VI

A Memorandum on a Practicable Soviet of Technicians

I t *is the purpose of this memorandum to show, in an* objective way, that under existing circumstances there need be no fear, and no hope, of an effectual revolutionary overturn in America, such as would unsettle the established order and unseat those Vested Interests that now control the country's industrial system. In an earlier paper (Chapter IV, pages 96 *et seq.*) it has been argued that no effectual move in the direction of such an overturn can be made except on the initiative and under the direction of the country's technicians, taking action in common and on a concerted plan. Notoriously, no move of this nature has been made hitherto, nor is there evidence that anything of the kind has been contemplated by the technicians. They still are consistently loyal, with something more than a hired-man's loyalty, to the established order of commercial profit and absentee ownership. And any adequate plan of concerted action, such as would be required for the enterprise in question, is not a small matter that can be arranged between two days.

Any plan of action that shall hope to meet the requirements of the case in any passable fashion must necessarily have the benefit of mature deliberation among the technicians who are competent to initiate such an enterprise; it must engage the intelligent co-operation of several thousand technically trained men scattered over the face of the country, in one industry and another; must carry out a passably complete castration of the country's industrial forces; must set up practicable organization tables covering the country's industry in some detail,—energy-resources, materials, and man power; and it must also engage the aggressive support of the trained men at work in transportation, mining, and the greater mechanical industries. These are initial requirements, indispensable to the initiation of any enterprise of the kind in such an industrial country as America; and so soon as this is called to mind it will be realised that any fear of an effectual move in this direction at present is quite chimerical. So that, in fact, it may be set down without a touch of ambiguity that absentee ownership is secure, just yet.

Therefore, to show conclusively and in an objective way how remote any contingency of this nature still is, it is here proposed to set out in a summary fashion the main lines which any such concerted plan of action would have to follow, and what will of necessity be the manner of organization which alone can hope to take over the industrial system, following the eventual abdication or dispossession of the Vested Interests and their absentee owners. And, by way of parenthesis, it is always the self-made though reluctant abdication of the Vested Interests and their absentee owners, rather than their forcible dispossession, that is to be looked for as a reasonably probable event in the calculable future. It should, in effect, cause no surprise to find that they will, in a sense, eliminate themselves, by letting go quite involuntarily after the industrial situation gets quite beyond their control. In fact, they have, in the present difficult juncture, already sufficiently shown their unfitness to take care of the country's material welfare,—which is after all the only ground on which they can set up a colorable claim to their vested rights. At the same time something like an opening bid for a bargain of abdication has already come in from more than one quarter. So that a discontinuance of the existing system of absentee ownership, on one plan or another, is no longer to be considered a purely speculative novelty; and an objective canvass of the manner of organization that is to be looked to to take the place of the control now exercised by the Vested Interests—in the event of their prospective abdication—should accordingly have some present interest, even apart from its bearing on the moot question of any forcible disruption of the established system of absentee ownership.

As a matter of course, the powers and duties of the incoming directorate will be of a technological nature, in the main if not altogether; inasmuch as the purpose of its coming into control is the care of the community's material welfare by a more competent management of the country's industrial system. It may be added that even in the unexpected event that the contemplated overturn should, in the beginning, meet with armed opposition from the partisans of the old order, it will still be true that the duties of the incoming directorate will be of a technological character, in the main; inasmuch as warlike operations are also now substantially a matter of technology, both in the immediate conduct of hostilities and in the still more urgent work of material support and supply.

The incoming industrial order is designed to correct the shortcomings of the old. The duties and powers of the incoming directorate will accordingly converge on those points in the administration of industry where the old order has most signally fallen short; that is to say, on the due allocation of resources and a consequent full and reasonably proportioned employment of the available equipment and man power; on the avoidance of waste and duplication of work; and on an equitable and sufficient supply of goods and services to consumers. Evidently the most immediate and most urgent work to be taken over by the incoming directorate is that for want of which under the old order the industrial system has been working slack and at cross purposes; that is to say the due allocation of available resources, in power, equipment, and materials, among the greater primary industries. For this necessary work of allocation there has been substantially no provision under the old order.

To carry on this allocation, the country's transportation system must be placed at the disposal of the same staff that has the work of allocation to do; since, under modern conditions, any such allocation will take effect only by use of the transportation system. But, by the same token, the effectual control of the distribution of goods to consumers will also necessarily fall into the same hands; since the traffic in consumable goods is also a matter of transportation, in the main.

On these considerations, which would only be reinforced by a more detailed inquiry into the work to be done, the central directorate will apparently take the shape of a loosely tripartite executive council, with power to act in matters of industrial administration; the council to include technicians whose qualifications enable them to be called Resource Engineers, together with similarly competent spokesmen of the transportation system and of the distributive traffic in finished products and services. With a view to efficiency and expedition, the executive council will presumably not be a numerous body; although its staff of intelligence and advice may be expected to be fairly large, and it will be guided by current consultation with the accredited spokesmen (deputies, commissioners, executives, or whatever they may be called) of the several main subdivisions of productive industry, transportation, and distributive traffic.

Armed with these powers and working in due consultation with a sufficient ramification of subcenters and local councils, this industrial directorate should be in a position to avoid virtually all unemployment of serviceable equipment and man power on the one hand, and all local or seasonal scarcity on the other hand. The main line of duties indicated by the character of the work incumbent on the directorate, as well as the main line of qualifications in its personnel, both executive and advisory, is such as will call for the services of Production Engineers, to use a term which is coming into use. But it is also evident that in its continued work of planning and advisement the directorate will require the services of an appreciable number of consulting economists; men who are qualified to be called Production Economists.

The profession now includes men with the requisite qualifications, although it cannot be said that the gild of economists is made up of such men in the main. Quite blamelessly, the economists have, by tradition and by force of commercial pressure, habitually gone in for a theoretical inquiry into the ways and means of salesmanship, financial traffic, and the distribution of income and property, rather than a study of the industrial system considered as a ways and means of producing goods and services. Yet there now are, after all, especially among the younger generation, an appreciable number, perhaps an adequate number, of economists who have learned that "business" is not "industry" and that investment is not production. And, here as always, the best is good enough, perforce.

"Consulting economists" of this order are a necessary adjunct to the personnel of the central directorate, because the technical training that goes to make a resource engineer, or a production engineer, or indeed a competent industrial expert in any line of specialization, is not of a kind to give him the requisite sure and facile insight into the play of economic forces at large; and as a matter of notorious fact, very few of the technicians have gone at all far afield to acquaint themselves with anything more to the point in this connection than the half-forgotten commonplaces of the old order. The "consulting economist" is accordingly necessary to cover an otherwise uncovered joint in the new articulation of things. His place in the scheme is analogous to the part which legal counsel now plays in the manœuvres of diplomatists and statesmen; and the discretionary personnel of the incoming directorate are to be, in effect, something in the way of industrial statesmen under the new order.

There is also a certain general reservation to be made with regard to personnel, which may conveniently be spoken of at this point. To avoid persistent confusion and prospective defeat, it will be necessary to exclude from all positions of trust and executive responsibility all persons who have been trained for business or who have had experience in business undertakings of the larger sort. This will apply generally, throughout the administrative scheme, although it will apply more imperatively as regards the responsible personnel of the directorate, central and subordinate, together with their staff of intelligence and advice, wherever judgment and insight are essential. What is wanted is training in the ways and means of productive industry, not in the ways and means of salesmanship and profitable investment.

By force of habit, men trained to a businesslike view of what is right and real will be irretrievably biassed against any plan of production and distribution that is not drawn in terms of commercial profit and loss and does not provide a margin of free income to go to absentee owners. The personal exceptions to the rule are apparently very few. But this one point is after all of relatively minor consequence. What is more to the point in the same connection is that the commercial bias induced by their training in businesslike ways of thinking leaves them incapable of anything like an effectual insight into the use of resources or the needs and aims of productive industry, in any other terms than those of commercial profit and loss. Their units and standards of valuation and accountancy are units and standards of price, and of private gain in terms of price; whereas for any scheme of productive industry which runs, not on salesmanship and earnings, but on tangible performances and tangible benefit to the community at large, the valuations and accountancy of salesmanship and earnings are misleading. With the best and most benevolent intentions, men so trained will unavoidably make their appraisals of production and their disposition of productive forces in the only practical terms with which they are familiar, the terms of commercial accountancy; which is the same as saying, the accountancy of absentee ownership and free income; all of which it is the abiding purpose of the projected plan to displace. For the purposes of this projected new order of production, therefore, the experienced and capable business men are at the best to be rated as well-intentioned deaf-mute blind men. Their wisest judgment and sincerest endeavors become meaningless and misguided so soon as the controlling purpose of industry shifts from the footing of profits on absentee investment to that of a serviceable output of goods.

All this abjuration of business principles and businesslike sagacity may appear to be a taking of precautions about a vacant formality; but it is as well to recall that by trained propensity and tradition the business men, great and small, are after all, each in their degree, lieutenants of those Vested Interests which the projected organization of industry is designed to displace,—schooled in their tactics and marching under their banners. The experience of the war administration and its management of industry by help of the business men during the past few years goes to show what manner of industrial wisdom is to be looked for where capable and well-intentioned business men are called in to direct industry with a view to maximum production and economy. For its responsible personnel the administration has uniformly drawn on experienced business men, preferably men of successful experience in Big Business; that is to say, trained men with a shrewd eye to the main chance. And the tale of its adventures, so far as a businesslike reticence has allowed them to become known, is an amazing comedy of errors; which runs to substantially the same issue whether it is told of one or another of the many departments, boards, councils, commissions, and administrations, that have had this work to do.

Notoriously, this choice of personnel has with singular uniformity proved to be of doubtful advisability, not to choose a harsher epithet. The policies pursued, doubtless with the best and most sagacious intentions of which this business-like personnel have been capable, have uniformly resulted in the safeguarding of investments and the allocation of commercial profits; all the while that the avowed aim of it all, and doubtless the conscientious purpose of the businesslike administrators, has been quantity production of essential goods. The more that comes to light, the more visible becomes the difference between the avowed purpose and the tangible performance. Tangible performance in the way of productive industry is precisely what the business men do not know how to propose, but it is also that on which the possible success of any projected plan of overturn will always rest. Yet it is also to be remarked that even the reluctant and blindfold endeavors of these businesslike administrators to break away from their life-long rule of reasonable earnings, appear to have resulted in a very appreciably increased industrial output per unit of man power and equipment employed. That such was the outcome under the war administration is presumably due in great part to the fact that the business men in charge were unable to exercise so strict a control over the working force of technicians and skilled operatives during that period of stress.

And here the argument comes in touch with one of the substantial reasons why there need be no present fear of a revolutionary overturn. By settled habit, the American population are quite unable to see their way to entrust any appreciable responsibility to any other than business men; at the same time that such a move of overturn can hope to succeed only if it excludes the business men from all positions of responsibility. This sentimental deference of the American people to the sagacity of its business men is massive, profound, and alert. So much so that it will take harsh and protracted experience to remove it, or to divert it sufficiently for the purpose of any revolutionary diversion. And more particularly, popular sentiment in this country will not tolerate the assumption of responsibility by the technicians, who are in the popular apprehension conceived to be a somewhat fantastic brotherhood of over-specialized cranks, not to be trusted out of sight except under the restraining hand of safe and sane business men. Nor are the technicians themselves in the habit of taking a greatly different view of their own case. They still feel themselves, in the nature of things, to fall into place as employes of those enterprising business men who are, in the nature of things, elected to get something for nothing. Absentee ownership is secure, just yet. In time, with sufficient provocation, this popular frame of mind may change, of course; but it is in any case a matter of an appreciable lapse of time.

Even such a scant and bare outline of generalities as has been hastily sketched above will serve to show that any effectual overturn of the established order is not a matter to be undertaken out of hand, or to be manœuvred into shape by makeshifts after the initial move has been made. There is no chance without deliberate preparations from beforehand. There are two main lines of preparations that will have to be taken care of by any body of men who may contemplate such a move: (a) An inquiry into existing conditions and into the available ways and means; and (b) the setting up of practicable organization tables and a survey of the available personnel. And bound up with this work of preparation, and conditioning it, provision must also be made for the growth of such a spirit of teamwork as will be ready to undertake and undergo this critical adventure. All of which will take time.

It will be necessary to investigate and to set out in a convincing way what are the various kinds and lines of waste that are necessarily involved in the present businesslike control of industry; what are the abiding causes of these wasteful and obstructive practices; and what economies of management and production will become practicable on the elimination of the present businesslike control. This will call for diligent teamwork on the part of a suitable group of economists and engineers, who will have to be drawn together by self-selection on the basis of a common interest in productive efficiency, economical use of resources, and an equitable distribution of the consumable output. Hitherto no such self-selection of competent persons has visibly taken place, and the beginnings of a plan for team-work in carrying on such an inquiry are yet to be made.

In the course of this contemplated inquiry and on the basis afforded by its findings there is no less serious work to be done in the way of deliberation and advisement, among the members of the group in question and in consultation with outside technological men who know what can best be done with the means in hand, and whose interest in things drives them to dip into the same gainless adventure. This will involve the setting up of organization tables to cover the efficient use of the available resources and equipment, as well as to re-organize the traffic involved in the distribution of the output.

By way of an illustrative instance, to show by an example something of what the scope and method of this inquiry and advisement will presumably be like, it may be remarked that under the new order the existing competitive commercial traffic engaged in the distribution of goods to consumers will presumably fall away, in the main, for want of a commercial incentive. It is well known, in a general way, that the present organization of this traffic, by wholesale and retail merchandising, involves a very large and very costly duplication of work, equipment, stock, and personnel,— several hundred per cent. more than would be required by an economically efficient management of the traffic on a reasonable plan. In looking for a way out of the present extremely wasteful merchandising traffic, and in working out organization tables for an equitable and efficient distribution of goods to consumers, the experts in the case will, it is believed, be greatly helped out by detailed information on such existing organizations as, e.g., the distributing system of the

Chicago Packers, the chain stores, and the mail-order houses. These are commercial organizations, of course, and as such they are managed with a view to the commercial gain of their owners and managers; but they are at the same time designed to avoid the ordinary wastes of the ordinary retail distribution, for the benefit of their absentee owners. There are not a few object-lessons of economy of this practical character to be found among the Vested Interests; so much so that the economies which result from them are among the valuable capitalized assets of these business concerns.

This contemplated inquiry will, of course, also be useful in the way of publicity; to show, concretely and convincingly, what are the inherent defects of the present businesslike control of industry, why these defects are inseparable from a businesslike control under existing circumstances, and what may fairly be expected of an industrial management which takes no account of absentee ownership. The ways and means of publicity to be employed is a question that plainly cannot profitably be discussed beforehand, so long as the whole question of the contemplated inquiry itself has little more than a speculative interest; and much the same will have to be said as to the scope and detail of the inquiry, which will have to be determined in great part by the interest and qualifications of the men who are to carry it on. Nothing but provisional generalities could at all confidently be sketched into its program until the work is in hand.

The contemplated eventual shift to a new and more practicable system of industrial production and distribution has been here spoken of as a "revolutionary overturn" of the established order. This flagitious form of words is here used chiefly because the Guardians of the established order are plainly apprehensive of something sinister that can be called by no gentler name, rather than with the intention of suggesting that extreme and subversive measures alone can now save the life of the underlying population from the increasingly disserviceable rule of the Vested Interests. The

move which is here discussed in a speculative way under
this sinister form of words, as a contingency to be guarded
against by fair means and foul, need, in effect, be nothing
spectacular; assuredly it need involve no clash of arms or
fluttering of banners, unless, as is beginning to seem likely,
the Guardians of the old order should find that sort of thing
expedient. In its elements, the move will be of the simplest
and most matter-of-fact character; although there will doubtless be many intricate adjustments to be made in detail. In
principle, all that is necessarily involved is a disallowance of
absentee ownership; that is to say, the disestablishment of an
institution which has, in the course of time and change,
proved to be noxious to the common good. The rest will
follow quite simply from the cancelment of this outworn and
footless vested right.

By absentee ownership, as the term applies in this connection, is here to be understood the ownership of an industrially useful article by any person or persons who are not
habitually employed in the industrial use of it. In this connection, office work of a commercial nature is not rated as
industrial employment. A corollary of some breadth follows
immediately, although it is so obvious an implication of the
main proposition that it should scarcely need explicit statement: An owner who is employed in the industrial use of a
given parcel of property owned by him, will still be an "absentee owner," within the meaning of the term, in case he is
not the only person habitually employed in its use. A further
corollary follows, perhaps less obvious at first sight, but no
less convincing on closer attention to the sense of the terms
employed: Collective ownership, of the corporate form, that
is to say ownership by a collectivity instituted *ad hoc*, also
falls away as being unavoidably absentee ownership, within
the meaning of the term. It will be noted that all this does
not touch joint ownership of property held in undivided interest by a household group and made use of by the members
of the household conjointly. It is only in so far as the house-

hold is possessed of useful property not made use of by its members, or not made use of without hired help, that its ownership of such property falls within the meaning of the term, absentee ownership. To be sufficiently explicit, it may be added that the cancelment of absentee ownership as here understood will apply indiscriminately to all industrially useful objects, whether realty or personalty, whether natural resources, equipment, banking capital, or wrought goods in stock.

As an immediate consequence of this cancelment of absentee ownership it should seem to be altogether probable that industrially useful articles will presently cease to be used for purposes of ownership, that is to say for purposes of private gain; although there might be no administrative interference with such use. Under the existing state of the industrial arts, neither the natural resources drawn on for power and materials nor the equipment employed in the great and controlling industries are of a nature to lend themselves to any other than absentee ownership; and these industries control the situation, so that private enterprise for gain on a small scale would scarcely find a suitable market. At the same time the inducement to private accumulation of wealth at the cost of the community would virtually fall away, inasmuch as the inducement to such accumulation now is in nearly all cases an ambition to come in for something in the way of absentee ownership. In effect, other incentives are a negligible quantity. Evidently, the secondary effects of such cancelment will go far, in more than one direction, but evidently, too, there could be little profit in endeavoring to follow up these ulterior contingencies in extended speculations here.

As to the formalities, of legal complexion, that would be involved in such a disallowance of absentee ownership, they need also be neither large nor intricate; at least not in their main incidence. It will in all probability take the shape of a cancelment of all corporation securities, as an initial move. Articles of partnership, evidences of debt, and other legal instruments which now give title to property not in hand or not in use by the owner, will be voided by the same act. In all probability this will be sufficient for the purpose.

This act of disallowance may be called subversive and revolutionary; but while there is no intention here to offer anything in the way of exculpation, it is necessary to an objective appraisal of the contemplated move to note that the effect of such disallowance would be subversive or revolutionary only in a figurative sense of the words. It would all of it neither subvert nor derange any substantial mechanical contrivance or relation, nor need it materially disturb the relations, either as workman or as consumer of goods and services, of any appreciable number of persons now engaged in productive industry. In fact, the disallowance will touch nothing more substantial than a legal make-believe. This would, of course, be serious enough in its consequences to those classes—called the kept classes—whose livelihood hangs on the maintenance of this legal make-believe. So, likewise, it would vacate the occupation of the "middleman," which likewise turns on the maintenance of this legal make-believe; which gives "title" to that to which one stands in no material relation.

Doubtless, hardship will follow thick and fast, among those classes who are least inured to privation; and doubtless all men will agree that it is a great pity. But this evil is, after all, a side issue, as regards the present argument, which has to do with nothing else than the practicability of the scheme. So it is necessary to note that, however detrimental to the special interests of the absentee owners this move may be, yet it will not in any degree derange or diminish those material facts that constitute the ways and means of productive industry; nor will it in any degree enfeeble or mutilate that joint stock of technical knowledge and practice that constitutes the intellectual working force of the industrial system. It does not directly touch the material facts of industry, for better or worse. In this sense it is a completely idle matter, in its immediate incidence, whatever its secondary consequences may be believed to be.

But there is no doubt that a proposal to disallow absentee ownership will shock the moral sensibilities of many persons; more particularly the sensibilities of the absentee owners. To avoid the appearance of willful neglect, therefore, it is necessary to speak also of the "moral aspect." There is no intention here to argue the moral merits of this contemplated disallowance of absentee ownership; or to argue for or against such a move, on moral or other grounds. Absentee ownership is legally sound today. Indeed, as is well known, the Constitution includes a clause which specially safeguards its security. If, and when, the law is changed, in this respect, what is so legal today will of course cease to be legal. There is, in fact, not much more to be said about it; except that, in the last resort, the economic moralities wait on the economic necessities. The economic-moral sense of the American community today runs unequivocally to the effect that absentee ownership is fundamentally and eternally right and good; and it should seem reasonable to believe that it will continue to run to that effect for some time yet.

There has lately been some irritation and fault-finding with what is called "profiteering" and there may be more or less uneasy discontent with what is felt to be an unduly disproportionate inequality in the present distribution of income; but apprehensive persons should not lose sight of the main fact that absentee ownership after all is the idol of every true American heart. It is the substance of things hoped for and the reality of things not seen. To achieve (or to inherit) a competency, that is to say to accumulate such wealth as will assure a "decent" livelihood in industrial *absentia*, is the universal, and universally laudable, ambition of all who have reached years of discretion; but it all means the same thing—to get something for nothing, at any cost. Similarly universal is the awestruck deference with which the larger absentee owners are looked up to for guidance and example. These substantial citizens are the ones who have "made good," in the popular apprehension. They are the great and good men whose lives "all remind us we can make our lives sublime, etc."

This commercialized frame of mind is a sturdy outgrowth of many generations of consistent training in the pursuit of the main chance; it is second nature, and there need be no fear that it will allow the Americans to see workday facts in any other than its own perspective, just yet. The most tenacious factor in any civilization is a settled popular frame of mind, and to this abiding American frame of mind absentee ownership is the controlling center of all the economic realities.

So, having made plain that all this argument on a practicable overturn of the established order has none but a speculative interest, the argument can go on to consider what will be the nature of the initial move of overturn which is to break with the old order of absentee ownership and set up a régime of workmanship governed by the country's technicians.

As has already been called to mind, repeatedly, the effective management of the industrial system at large is already in the hands of the technicians, so far as regards the work actually done; but it is all under the control of the Vested Interests, representing absentee owners, so far as regards its failure to work. And the failure is, quite reasonably, attracting much attention lately. In this two-cleft, or bicameral, administration of industry, the technicians may be said to represent the community at large in its industrial capacity, or in other words the industrial system as a going concern; whereas the business men speak for the commercial interest of the absentee owners, as a body which holds the industrial community in usufruct. It is the part of the technicians, between them, to know the country's available resources, in mechanical power and equipment; to know and put in practice the joint stock of technological knowledge which is indispensable to industrial production; as well as to know and take care of the community's habitual need and use of consumable goods. They are, in effect, the general staff of production engineers, under whose surveillance the required output of goods and services is produced and distributed to the consumers. Whereas it is the part of the business men to know what rate and volume of production and distribution will best serve the commercial interest of the absentee owners, and to put this commercial knowledge in practice by nicely limiting production and distribution of the output to such a rate and volume as their commercial traffic will bear—that is to say, what will yield the largest net income to the absentee owners in terms of price. In this work of sagaciously retarding industry the captains of industry necessarily work at cross purposes, among themselves, since the traffic is of a competitive nature.

Accordingly, in this two-cleft arrangement of administrative functions, it is the duty of the technicians to plan the work and to carry it on; and it is the duty of the captains of industry to see that the work will benefit none but the captains and their associated absentee owners, and that it is not pushed beyond the salutary minimum which their commercial traffic will bear. In all that concerns the planning and execution of the work done, technicians necessarily take the initiative and exercise the necessary creative surveillance and direction; that being what they, and they alone, are good for; whereas the businesslike deputies of the absentee owners sagaciously exercise a running veto power over the technicians and their productive industry. They are able effectually to exercise this commercially sagacious veto power by the fact that the technicians are, in effect, their employes, hired to do their bidding and fired if they do not; and perhaps no less by this other fact, that the technicians have hitherto been working piecemeal, as scattered individuals

under their master's eye; they have hitherto not drawn together on their own ground and taken counsel together as a
general staff of industry, to determine what had best be done
and what not. So that they have hitherto figured in the conduct of the country's industrial enterprise only as a technological extension of the business men's grasp on the commercial
main chance.

Yet, immediately and unremittingly, the technicians
and their advice and surveillance are essential to any work
whatever in those great primary industries on which the
country's productive systems run, and which set the pace for
all the rest. And it is obvious that so soon as they shall draw
together, in a reasonably inclusive way, and take common
counsel as to what had best be done, they are in a position
to say what work shall be done and to fix the terms on which
it is to be done. In short, so far as regards the technical requirements of the case, the situation is ready for a self-se-
lected, but inclusive, Soviet of technicians to take over the
economic affairs of the country and to allow and disallow
what they may agree on; provided always that they live
within the requirements of that state of the industrial arts
whose keepers they are, and provided that their pretensions
continue to have the support of the industrial rank and file;
which comes near saying that their Soviet must consistently
and effectually take care of the material welfare of the underlying population.

Now, this revolutionary posture of the present state of
the industrial arts may be undesirable, in some respects, but
there is nothing to be gained by denying the fact. So soon—
but only so soon—as the engineers draw together, take common counsel, work out a plan of action, and decide to disallow absentee ownership out of hand, that move will have
been made. The obvious and simple means of doing it is a
conscientious withdrawal of efficiency; that is to say the
general strike, to include so much of the country's staff of
technicians as will suffice to incapacitate the industrial sys-

tem at large by their withdrawal, for such time as may be required to enforce their argument.

In its elements, the project is simple and obvious, but its working out will require much painstaking preparation, much more than appears on the face of this bald statement; for it also follows from the present state of the industrial arts and from the character of the industrial system in which modern technology works out, that even a transient failure to make good in the conduct of productive industry will result in a precipitated collapse of the enterprise.

By themselves alone, the technicians can, in a few weeks, effectually incapacitate the country's productive industry sufficiently for the purpose. No one who will dispassionately consider the technical character of this industrial system will fail to recognize that fact. But so long as they have not, at least, the tolerant consent of the population at large, backed by the aggressive support of the trained working force engaged in transportation and in the greater primary industries, they will be substantially helpless to set up a practicable working organization on the new footing; which is the same as saying that they will in that case accomplish nothing more to the purpose than a transient period of hardship and dissension.

Accordingly, if it be presumed that the production engineers are of a mind to play their part, there will be at least two main lines of subsidiary preparation to be taken care of before any overt move can reasonably be undertaken: (a) An extensive campaign of inquiry and publicity, such as will bring the underlying population to a reasonable understanding of what it is all about; and (b) the working-out of a common understanding and a solidarity of sentiment between the technicians and the working force engaged in transportation and in the greater underlying industries of the system: to which is to be added as being nearly indispensable from the outset, an active adherence to this plan on the part of the trained workmen in the great generality of the mechanical industries. Until these prerequisites are taken care of, any project for the overturn of the established order of absentee ownership will be nugatory.

By way of conclusion it may be recalled again that, just yet, the production engineers are a scattering lot of fairly contented subalterns, working piecemeal under orders from the deputies of the absentee owners; the working force of the great mechanical industries, including transportation, are still nearly out of touch and out of sympathy with the technical men, and are bound in rival trade organizations whose sole and self-seeking interest converges on the full dinner-pail; while the underlying population are as nearly uninformed on the state of things as the Guardians of the Vested Interests, including the commercialized newspapers, can manage to keep them, and they are consequently still in a frame of mind to tolerate no substantial abatement of absentee ownership; and the constituted authorities are competently occupied with maintaining the status quo. There is nothing in the situation that should reasonably flutter the sensibilities of the Guardians or of that massive body of well-to-do citizens who make up the rank and file of absentee owners, just yet.

WITHDRAWN
FROM STOCK
QMUL LIBRARY

WITHDRAWN
FROM STOCK
QMUL LIBRARY